FEAR FREE

Graham Powell

on loan to
R.C.I.A.
St. Mary's
Paisley

Sovereign World

Scripture quotations in this volume are from the
New American Standard Bible, © The Lockman
Foundation, 1960, 1962, 1963, 1968, 1971, 1972,
1973, 1975, La Habra, California.

Sovereign World Ltd.
P. O. Box 17,
Chichester PO20 6RY
England

Printed and bound in Great Britain by
Courier International Ltd, Tiptree, Essex

ISBN 1 85240 015 3

Acknowledgements

To those who made valuable comments regarding the manuscript, most particularly, John Wiebe of Vancouver B.C., whose contribution has been invaluable.

To Shirley, my wife, for her willing assistance in the typings of the manuscript and for her constant love and support in the adventures of life we share together.

About the Author

Graham Powell was born in New Zealand. Before training as a school-teacher he spent time in the Mercantile
Marine. As a young man he was converted at a Youth
for Christ rally and soon became involved in Christian
service.

For more than twenty years, he and his wife Shirley
have been serving God together, in both evangelistic
and pastoral ministry in New Zealand, Australia and
Canada.

Currently they are involved in itinerant evangelistic
and teaching ministry in Canada and beyond, and travel
as a family with their two children. They are based in
British Columbia.

Graham and Shirley Powell conduct teaching
seminars and deliverance and healing services.

Inquiries as to the availability of their ministry should
be directed to:

Center Mountain Ministries,
P.O. Box 120, Westbridge,
B.C., VOH 2BO, Canada.

Contents

Chapter 1

The Reality of Fear

"PHOBIAS." The word in bold print on the front cover of NEWSWEEK caught my attention. Purchasing a copy I turned to the feature article and read the following caption; "THE FIGHT TO CONQUER FEAR: Phobias afflict millions of Americans — but new therapies are providing help."*

Newsweek called fear the disease of the decade. "What schizophrenia was to the 1960's, what depression and burnout were to the 1970's, phobias are to the 1980's."* The article went on to state that one in nine American adults harbour some kind of phobia, only alcoholism being a more widespread mental-health problem. "This statistic becomes even more impressive when one considers that many alcoholics are suspected of being phobics who merely mask their problem with drink."*

Anyone who counsels people on a regular basis will probably agree that one in nine underestimates the severity of the problem. Indeed, most people, if they are honest, must admit that they struggle to varying degrees with fear in one form or another. No one knows how many people walk into an elevator with a degree of anxiety, how many are impeded in everyday activities

*© 1984, by Newsweek, Inc. All Rights Reserved. Reprinted by Permission.

by the fear of heights, how many are over-sensitised in their relationships through the fear of being rejected. Although hidden behind brave exteriors, fears of every description stalk and grip multitudes.

Unfriendly Skies

Captioned "Unfriendly Skies," the Newsweek article concluded with a glimpse of aerophobia, and quoted a 1977 Boeing survey, that estimated twenty-five million Americans had a fear of flying. These statistics embraced many celebrities. "Ronald Reagan's political ambitions had to overcome his aerophobia before he could run for governor of sprawling California, and soul singer Aretha Franklin recently cancelled several concert dates to avoid leaving terra firma. The aerophobe wears many faces: some run down the aisle screaming, "Stop the plane," as it taxis toward the runway; others endure the trip only through an alcohol- or sedative-induced haze. Many fearful fliers are in fact terrified of being shut up in a confined space thousands of feet above the ground; ex-Oakland Raiders head coach and claustrophobe John Madden, for example, takes Amtrak coast to coast to do his TV broadcasts rather than watch the stewardess close those doors."*

Nuclear Warfare

The fear of nuclear war and all its accompanying devastation is a fear that preoccupies many. Recently we ministered to someone from The Netherlands who had migrated to New Zealand because of the fear of nuclear war and nuclear fallout. This person thought that "down under" New Zealand would be one of the safest places to be in the event of such a conflagration.

Chernobyl alerted the world to the danger and destruction of nuclear radiation upon both people and their lands. Being in Europe at the time of the nuclear accident we witnessed first hand the anxiety aroused by this Soviet disaster.

Animal Kingdom

Fear is not confined to the human race alone, but is widespread amongst the animal kingdom as well — animals afraid of animals, animals afraid of man.

As a family we formerly lived in a Canadian wilderness environment where we had many opportunities to view wild life in its natural habitat. While walking near our home one day, I noticed a number of coyotees in the distance. Concealing myself behind some logs on the edge of a hay-field, I watched as seven coyotees played together. Unaware of my presence, they gradually came closer until they were only fifteen to twenty feet away. A breeze had been carrying my scent in the opposite direction, but, when the first coyote, passing directly in front of me, became aware of my presence, it leapt into the air and streaked away in terror. The others wondered what had upset their companion. Soon a second coyote scented me as well, and it, too, jumped and fled. As one by one the others went through the same antics it became only too apparent that fear is common to the animal kingdom too.

Isaiah the prophet spoke of a day when fear will be absent from both man and beast (Isaiah 11:6). When will this be a reality? When Jesus Christ returns to this earth to rule the nations. Then there will be peace among nations, within communities, in the family unit, and in the heart of individuals. Then there will be peace amongst animals as well as an absence of fear between man and beast. In that day men also will live in peace with each other. What a day that will be!

Fear Not

Recognising the devastating effect of fear upon man, the Bible has much to say on the subject. Indeed, on numerous occasions God admonishes His people to "fear not". Why is this command so often repeated? Because God knows how real fear is to man, and how we need to be alerted to trust Him in the midst of every circumstance and situation.

Transformation

Some months back a young woman approached us after a meeting we had conducted. She asked if we remembered her, and after some deliberation I said, "Yes," and spoke her name. The reason that I did not recognise her immediately was the wonderful change that had taken place since she had been prayed for five years previously. At that time her face and arms bore slashmarks because of attempts at self destruction, and she was gripped by numerous fears, describing herself as being bound on the inside by chains. But here she was, confident, smiling and giving thanks to Jesus Christ who had brought about such a wonderful transformation.

Perhaps you too know the reality of those inward chains from which there seems no way of escape. You too know the reality of constant torment. How wonderful to know that God is able and willing to release us from every affliction and to enable us to be fear free.

Chapter 2

Types of Fear

All fear however, does not fit into the category of affliction. Fears fall into three areas, two being positive while one is definitely negative. It is the latter that we are concerned with, but it will be helpful to be aware of the positive fears as well. The first we will call "Natural Fear".

Natural Fear

God has placed within man the instinct of preservation. There is then, a kind of fear that is a natural reaction to threatening circumstances and situations of impending danger. At such times, the body pumps adrenalin into the bloodstream, releasing a sudden and super burst of mental and physical energy to face and combat danger.

While living in a wilderness community we faced the hazard of fire which had previously destroyed and damaged a number of buildings. At a time when no men were working in the immediate vicinity, the roof of the school caught fire. Fortunately it was noticed by one of the teachers and the fire alarm was sounded. Instantly the adrenalin glands began to do their work in students and teachers, and, with the reaction of fear, came special alertness. One teenage student leapt from the ground directly onto the school roof and began to douse the flames. When others tried to perform such a feat they were unable. Fortunately the fire was soon put out. Looking back, the young man wondered how he ever got onto the roof as he did. Admittedly, a pile of snow assisted his ascent, but it was obvious to everyone that an unusual burst of strength enabled him to do what he normally could not have done.

Perhaps you can look back on an experience in your life, when you too experienced this temporary surge of alertness and energy that helped you, or perhaps even saved your life. It is a positive fear. It is life preserving. However, when this condition of alert is maintained for too long a period of time, danger to the physical system can result. Indeed, a door can be opened to another dimension of fear, as we shall discover.

Let us consider now what we term "Necessary Fear."

Necessary Fear

This fear too, is life saving. The Bible calls it the "fear of God," since it is born out of awe, wonder and reverence for God. This fear should fill the hearts of all men as they consider the greatness of the Creator of the Universe. God is the Source of Creation. He is the Sustainer of all things. He is the God of Justice who will judge all men for their deeds.

Sometimes I have tried to put myself in God's position. How would I feel as the Creator if I had made the

Universe; if I had made a tiny planet called Earth; if I had made an infinitesimal speck of life called man, and purposed that this creature should be related to me as not only the Source of its being, but the Sustainer of its life? How would I feel were I to be neglected, rejected and even mocked and cursed? What would be my response, seeing these creatures, for whom I had such high purposes, denying even my existence? How would you feel if you were God? How do you think God must feel?

Personal Encounter

Prior to yielding my life to Jesus Christ, God's Son, as Lord and Saviour, I experienced a period in which I now realise the fear of the Lord came upon me. During that time, without anyone speaking to me about God, a sense of awe gripped my heart. Walking under the clear heavens of the Southern Hemisphere, I was strangely aware that the starry expanse was created by God and that one could know Him personally. At the same time I felt so unclean and so far from Him.

Not knowing how to find God, I went to a nearby church three times during those days, and, with no human observers, cried out to God to save me. A sense of impending judgment gripped me, and I was somehow aware that if I died I was going to Hell. Prostrating myself on the floor, I earnestly cried out to God, pleading that my sins be forgiven. On the third occasion, in desperation, I told the Lord that if He would forgive me my sins, I would be a missionary should that be His desire for me.

This awareness of the awesomeness of God and the sense of eternal judgment prepared my heart to receive the Gospel message, something that transpired shortly afterwards at a Youth For Christ rally. The evangelist spoke on the Second Coming of Christ to this earth as Judge. Such a message I had never heard in my church upbringing. It was completely new. As I sat in my seat, with the preacher still speaking, I lifted my heart to God. Darkness engulfed me. It was as if I was standing on the edge of a diving board about to dive into a pool of water. Because it was dark I couldn't see the water. Was there water in the pool? What would happen if I dived?

By faith I prayed and asked God's forgiveness. By faith I invited Jesus Christ to be the Saviour and Lord of my life. The moment I prayed the darkness lifted. A sense of cleanness filled me. God was no longer far away but near, even within me. Heaven was now my eternal destination. Life's outlook and direction completely changed for me as I surrendered fully to God's Son.

The "fear of the Lord" has never left me; instead, it has increased with the passing of time. Psalm 33:8 says, *"Let all the earth fear the Lord; Let all the inhabitants of the world stand in awe of Him."* Stand in "awe of Him"! Is this the response of most people? The Bible tells us, the *"fear of the Lord is clean"* (Psalm 19:9); is *"the beginning of wisdom"* (Psalm 111:10); is *"to hate evil"* (Proverbs 8:13); is *"a fountain of life"* (Proverbs 14:27). May there be, even as you read these words, a deep desire to be filled with this fear.

Isaiah, speaking of the coming Messiah, said prophetically that *"the spirit of knowledge and the fear of the Lord"* would rest on Jesus, and that *"He will delight in the fear of the Lord"* (Isaiah 11:2,3). Now we come to the third area we will call "Negative Fear."

Negative Fear

When Jeremiah spoke an oracle against Damascus, as recorded in Jeremiah 49:24, he said, *"Damascus has become helpless; she has turned away to flee, and panic has gripped her; distress and pangs have taken hold of her like a woman in childbirth."*

"To fasten upon, to bind," is the Hebrew description of the fear that grips. For years even to hear the words fear or peace mentioned would cause a gripping action inside me. Daily my body would become taut and stiff and I would shake visibly because of something binding me.

Fear brings torment. Torment of mind and emotions was my experience for years — before becoming a Christian — and after. Just accepting Jesus into our lives does not mean an automatic release from bondage in all areas of our lives. We must learn to enter into the inheritance Christ has purchased for us through His death and resurrection. In my search for peace of heart, which I knew was to be the experience of every Christian, I sought counsel from many. No one could help me, or even understand the intense inward struggle I endured. Today, however, light and understanding is flowing in many areas of Christendom as renewal and restoration is being experienced. Christians are rising up and taking the land of their lives for the Kingdom of God. This is a day of signs, wonders and miracles. As we learn to cooperate with the Spirit of God, we are discovering the reality of freedom from fears and all other afflictions of soul and body. God wants us to be totally free from negative fear.

Acknowledging Our Need

The first step to freedom is to acknowledge that we are bound by fear and that we need help. If we are not willing to acknowledge our need we may never experience liberty. Formerly I wondered why Jesus asked the blind beggar, Bartimaeus, *"What do you want Me to do for you?"* The need of this poor man was obvious to everyone in Jericho. Jesus, of course, recognised his need immediately, but wanted to hear a response from Bartimaeus' own lips. *"Lord I want to receive my sight!"* With that cry Jesus immediately healed him (Luke 18:40—42).

One of the very first ministers I sought help from as a young Christian asked me a question. "Do you have fear in your life?" I had sought help for a physical affliction and did not expect his question. So careful was I to keep under cover this area of need, I responded negatively. Looking back, I don't know if I was plainly dishonest, or if the very fear itself made me afraid to acknowledge its presence. Never again did I respond like that. It was hard on later occasions to admit areas of need or weakness, but so earnestly did I seek help that I opened up and endeavoured to be very honest with those from whom I sought counsel.

Are you prepared to be honest? Are you willing to

admit to God that fears grip your life? Are you prepared to open your heart to a godly counsellor and "say it like it is"? Often when people come for counsel they do not say what they need to say. Surface issues are shared at the expense of uncovering the real areas of need. This is often because of fear and embarrassment. Fortunately the Holy Spirit is gracious and is willing to reveal and penetrate to the real areas of need. Let us commence our walk into liberty from fear by acknowledging we need help.

Chapter 3

The Spiritual Nature of Fear

The fear that binds is more than a negative emotion, more than just a fixation, or a family character trait passed down from one generation to the next. FEAR IS A SPIRIT.

Spirits or evil spirits, as we should call them, for that is what they are, are living, intelligent beings who function in the spiritual realm. Their aim is to attack and grip us within our personalities, exerting an influence from one generation to the next, compounding our fears, robbing us of peace, and destroying us physically and spiritually. They function this way under the direction of their nefarious head, Satan, otherwise known as the Devil.

Satan has innumerable legions of evil spirits or demons — the terms are synonymous — carrying out his work of destruction amongst humanity. Spirits of fear have to be some of the most horrible of his underlings.

Satan, formerly called Lucifer, the shining-one (Isaiah 14:12), was one of the archangels of God before he rebelled and was cast out of Heaven along with other angels who joined him in his rebellion (Isaiah 14:12—15; Revelation 12:9). From the beginning of human history his influence has been evident. It was Satan who deceived Eve and enticed Adam to disobey God in the Garden of Eden. Since that time mankind has been subjected to the harassment and influence of satanic powers (Ephesians 2:1—3).

These evil spirits belong to the domain of darkness (Colossians 1:13). The Bible speaks of man's need to turn from darkness to light (Acts 26:18). The works of Satan are works of darkness whereas the Kingdom of God is characterised by light. Jesus said, *"I am the light of the world; he who follows Me shall not walk in darkness, but shall have the light of life"* (John 8:12).

Clashing of Kingdoms

The clash of two diametrically opposed kingdoms was visibly demonstrated when Jesus Christ commenced His earthly ministry anointed by the Holy Spirit (Acts 10:38). He was constantly casting out demons and thereby setting people free from spirit powers, often with dramatic manifestations as the light penetrated and dispelled the darkness.

Here are some verses from the first chapter of Mark's Gospel that demonstrate the might and power of Jesus to deliver the afflicted.

And they went into Capernaum; and immediately on the Sabbath He entered the synagogue and began to teach.
And they were amazed at His teaching; for He was teaching them as one having authority, and not as the scribes.

22

And just then there was in their synagogue a man with an unclean spirit; and he cried out,

saying, "What do we have to do with You, Jesus of Nazareth? Have You come to destroy us? I know who You are — the Holy One of God!"

And Jesus rebuked him, saying, "Be quiet, and come out of him!"

And throwing him into convulsions, the unclean spirit cried out with a loud voice, and came out of him.

And they were all amazed, so that they debated among themselves, saying, "What is this? A new teaching with authority! He commands even the unclean spirits, and they obey Him."   Mark 1:21—27

And when evening had come, after the sun had set, they began bringing to Him all who were ill and those who were demon-possessed.

And the whole city had gathered at the door.

And He healed many who were ill with various diseases, and cast out many demons; and He was not permitting the demons to speak, because they knew who He was.   Mark 1:32—34

And He went into their synagogues throughout all Galilee, preaching and casting out demons.

Mark 1:39

A distraught father came to Jesus with his tormented son, lamenting that from childhood the boy had been battered by a spirit that had thrown him into fire and water, endeavouring to destroy him. As the father cried out for help, Jesus, moved with compassion, went into action to bring deliverance.

And when Jesus saw that a crowd was rapidly gathering, He rebuked the unclean spirit, saying to it, "You

23

deaf and dumb spirit, I command you, come out of
him and do not enter him again."
And after crying out and throwing him into terrible
convulsions, it came out; and the boy became so much
like a corpse that most of them said, "He is dead!"
But Jesus took him by the hand and raised him; and
he got up. Mark 9:25—27

Spirits Have Names

Evil spirits have names that indicate their function. In
the above passage we read of Jesus casting out a deaf
and dumb spirit that had hindered the boy from hearing or speaking. Spirits of fear rob people of peace.
Spirits of infirmity afflict with sickness and disease.
Spirits of insanity take away soundness of mind, while
spirits of rebellion drive people to all kinds of lawless
deeds. Behind every sinful act are spirits that have first
enticed a person to sin and then seek to bind him in
it. Behind every negative emotion are spirits as well.
It is possible to experience fear or sorrow, for instance,
without being in a demonic bondage, but great, indeed,
is the number of those who are bound by spirits of fear,
sorrow, discouragement, depression, loneliness, rejection, hatred, lust, and disappointment to name only a
few. Men and women, however, do not have to remain
in bondage to these spirits. They can be set free!

Spirits Work in Groups

Spirits work in groups or families, and the larger the grouping of the same kind of spirit, the stronger the bondage area. The Bible talks of pulling down fortresses or strongholds (2 Corinthians 10:4) through the launching of spiritual weapons. These strongholds are established in the soul of man — in his mind, emotions and will, as well as in his body. The spirit of the non-Christian can be indwelt by demons, but since the Spirit of God indwells the Christian (1 Corinthians 3:16; John 3:6), demons attack him in the area of the soul and body.

Spirits Torment

On numerous occasions, as a little child, I would awaken in the night, aware of an unseen presence in my bedroom. I would be so intensely gripped with fear that there would be times when I was even unable to scream for help. The agony of such experiences was excruciating. Satan is no respecter of age. He will destroy helpless children, the aged, and anyone in between. His purpose is to bind, torment, and destroy; his ultimate aim, to usher men and women into a Christless eternity in Hell. Often I would experience nightmares, in which I would be falling, falling, falling never coming to the end. The Bible talks of the "bottomless pit" and I can well imagine what that may mean.

It was only as an adult, after some years of evangelistic ministry, that I became aware the origin of my fears was demonic. How blinded I had been. No one told me there were spiritual beings whose only purpose was to inspire fear. It never dawned on me that I was bound by demons just as people were in Bible days. Ignorance dominated me just as ignorance dominates so many people today.

Only as I came to acknowledge what evil spirits had done in my life, could I begin to deal with them in proven Bible methods. Actually, once demonic powers surfaced in my life, I still did not know how to deal with them. Only by a continued earnest seeking of God did understanding finally come, and that after much time had passed. My discoveries are fully shared in CHRISTIAN SET YOURSELF FREE.

Beating the Air?

In 1 Corinthians 9:25,26, Paul speaks of competitors striving after success in the sports arena .... *"I run in such a way, as not without aim; I box in such a way, as not beating the air."* As a teenager I was both an athlete and boxer; however because I did not recognise my fears as originating with evil spirits, and therefore had no way of dealing with them, I was as a boxer beating the air.

There are spirits of fear. They need to be recognised, acknowledged, and dealt with as such. Had I not recognised this, I would have gone through life forever struggling. No intelligent athlete seeks some imaginary finishing line. No skilful boxer goes into the ring blindfolded and expends all his energy beating the air, yet millions of people "beat the air" as they endeavour to overcome their fears because they fail to recognise the demonic dimension by which they have been snared.

When Paul wrote to Timothy (2 Timothy 1:7), he said, *"For God has not given us a spirit of timidity* (Greek deilia — timidity, fear), *but of power and love and discipline."*

Identifying the Source

The power of fear over lives was demonstrated when a friend approached me expressing his desire to start his own business. For as many as nine years he had served others in his area of expertise; yet, for much of this time he had wanted to be working independently. He was most able, but fearful, afraid he could not do it, afraid he might fail. Regulated by fear, this man's years were passing by, and the plans and purposes God had desired for him and his family were being thwarted, thwarted by spirits of fear.

Knowing the source of his debility, I laid hands on him and spoke the following commands. "In Jesus' Name, I bind every spirit of fear. All inferiority, all fear of failure, I render you powerless, you wicked spirits of darkness. Come out of him now. You have no legal right to afflict him. Go in Jesus' Name. Thank you Lord Jesus for releasing your servant. Thank you Lord for the ability to do your will without the restrictions of fear."

For a period of time we continued in warfare like this. On a second occasion we met again and continued to speak release in the Name of Jesus. During these encounters the strongholds began to crumble and this man discovered a releasing within himself. With the release came peace and confidence, and, shortly afterwards, he resigned his position and began his own company. Later he was to testify that the founding of his company and the success of his new business were a reality only because Jesus had set him free from fear.

Fears are spirits. How good it is to recognise that we can break free from these bondages. Firstly, however, we need to acknowledge our need of deliverance from fear; and, secondly, recognise that we are bound by spirits of fear.

Chapter 4

The Entrance of Fear

Some time ago we were travelling to Vancouver from Vancouver Island on one of the British Columbia Ferries. In the forward lounge we sat near a group of actors who were all very obviously gay. (Gays are not a liberated people at all, but are bound by spirits of homosexuality as well as other types of spirits). Two of the women spoke freely and loudly, so we heard much of their conversation. They spoke of their achievements, their travels, their aspirations and one finally said to the other, "I don't know who I am yet." Taking on different personality roles in a stage career would not help her quest, I'm sure, especially if she totally abandoned herself to fit the characters and parts she was required to play, but her expression of a quest for a personal identity is a quest engaged in by many.

Few persons know what it is to be completely free of demonic bondages, and consequently, have never discovered "who they really are". Most grow up unaware of the spiritual dimension that daily affects all of our lives. Because we don't "see" spirits we don't acknowledge their activity. Concealment is one of Satan's greatest advantages over us. Spirits of fear, camouflaged as feelings and emotions, lay hold of us and are accepted as a part of us. Because this is "just me", we don't expect to change, or know how to change, even if we want to.

Let us consider then, how fear gains entrance to our lives.

1. Separation from God

God made man to be fear free. It was not His intention that we should be afflicted by rebellion, disease, loneliness, fear, or death. Nor can we blame God for the afflictions in which we find ourselves. Adam, the first man, chose to disobey the clearcut directive of His Maker, and with that act of rebellion man became separated from God. The light within ceased, and darkness came. The joy of God's Presence was replaced by sorrow, and with the absence of peace came fear. Genesis 3:10 first mentions fear in the Bible .... *"I was afraid"* .... cried Adam, as he sought to hide from the all-seeing, all-knowing God. Fear then, is a natural consequence of our separation from God. It afflicts us all until we turn back to God and know a restoration of relationship with Him. This relationship is only possible through Jesus Christ the Son of God. Jesus is the only Way to the Father. Jesus' blood alone deals with our sin. Jesus is the only Saviour provided by God for mankind (Acts 4:10—12).

2. Exposure to the Powers of Darkness

When Adam rebelled against the Word of God, he abdicated his position of rulership over the earth. God had previously blessed Adam and Eve, saying, ... *"Be fruitful and multiply, and fill the earth, and subdue it; and rule over the fish of the sea and over the birds of the sky, and over every living thing that moves on the earth"* (Genesis 1:28).

With abdication and separation from God came exposure to the powers of darkness as Satan stepped in to control and dominate mankind. This too, brought a further dimension of fear because man was now alone to counteract an unseen enemy. Satan purposed to afflict man with every negative thing he could, though, as in the case of Job, Satan could only operate within the limits set for him by God.

Ephesians 6:10—18 speaks of the struggle we face as Christians, but also makes us aware of the armour available to us for protection and for warfare. Verse 12 says, *"For our struggle is not against flesh and blood, but against the rulers, against the powers, against the world forces of this darkness, against the spiritual forces of wickedness in the heavenly places."*

Because man turned from God and allowed Satan a place to function, millions of people through the centuries have lived in fear, not recognising the nature and source of these fears. In our Western society we are so ignorant of spiritual realities that we often deny the existence of God and of fallen spirit powers under Satan's command. But it is a different story in Third World nations; there people know only too well the reality of evil spirits. Much of their energy is spent appeasing them, worshipping them, seeking healing and prosperity from them. Great joy comes to these people when they yield to Jesus Christ, the Light of the World

31

and the Prince of Peace. Their experience of salvation can often be more meaningful because they know the depth of captivity from which they have been lifted.

No matter what your cultural background, if you have never yielded your life to Jesus Christ as Lord and Saviour, the Bible says you are under Satan's dominion. When Paul stood before King Agrippa, he declared that God had called him to labour amongst the Gentiles and to open their eyes so that they might turn from darkness to light and from the dominion of Satan to God (Acts 26:18).

You may feel secure in your religious heritage or your church membership. Leading a good life and attending services does not release you from Satan's dominion. Multitudes attend church regularly, but are going to Hell. Jesus said to the religious Pharisees of His day, *"You are of your father the devil, and you want to do the desires of your father. He was a murderer from the beginning, and does not stand in the truth, because there is no truth in him. Whenever he speaks a lie, he speaks from his own nature; for he is a liar, and the father of lies"* (John 8:44).

Previously I mentioned my own conversion experience. Even prior to the days leading up to an encounter with Christ, I had attended church sporadically. Satan had said to my mind that if I attended church all would be well as God would be pleased with me. He had nothing to fear in my attending the church I did for the Gospel was not preached from one year to the next, and consequently the kingdom of darkness was not being differentiated from the Kingdom of Light. Satan had lied to me. What I needed, what you need, is to meet Jesus Christ and surrender your life completely to Him.

Steps to Knowing God

If you are not sure of your allegiance to the Kingdom of Light, having never been restored to a relationship with God, you can come to Him right now by taking the following steps.

Firstly, you must be willing to repent of your sins. That means simply, to change your mind about the way you have been living and be willing to turn completely from sinful practices, occupations, friends, or anything that would entice you back to the old ways. Repentance is simply a cutting off of the past, of all that would be displeasing to God.

Secondly, you need to turn to the resurrected Christ acknowledging that a right relationship with God is only possible through Him. Jesus alone is the Saviour of the world. Jesus alone bridged the gulf between God and man by offering Himself as a perfect sacrifice for all of our sins. His blood alone is powerful enough to cleanse us from all defilement.

Thirdly, you need to confess your sins to God. Acknowledge you have fallen short of the requirements of His law and commandments. Acknowledge your guilt. Acknowledge your need of a Saviour.

Fourthly, yield your life to Jesus. Ask Him to be your Saviour. Confess Him as your Lord. Consciously yield every part of your being to the control of His presence and power. You are now no longer your own. You belong to Him.

Fifthly, confess audibly and publicly your identification with Christ as Lord and Saviour. Tell someone what you have done, particularly a fellow believer, who will rejoice with you and encourage you as you begin your walk with God.

Prayer of Salvation

Should you not know how to verbalise your response to God, make the following confession your honest prayer:

"Dear God, I come to you because I have made a decision to turn from my own way and from every sinful practice and association. I acknowledge that Jesus alone can save me because He died for me, taking the penalty I deserve for the breaking of Your commandments. I confess I have sinned against You, and ask You to forgive me for every sin I have committed, willfully, or in ignorance.

Jesus, I yield my life to You as Saviour and as Lord. Take me over from this moment on. Release me from all bondage. Fill me with Your Spirit. I am Yours Lord. I am Yours. I confess with my lips You are the Son of God with power. You have risen from the dead. You are Lord. You are my Lord."

Such a meaningful response completes the third step to freedom from fear. Already we have seen the importance of acknowledging our need of deliverance from fear, and acknowledging our bondage has its source in spirits of fear, but yielding to Jesus Christ as Lord and Saviour is paramount if we are to know true freedom.

3. Through the Parental Line

Every generation passes on to its progeny an inheritance which is both good and evil. One person has inherited artistic ability which has been a hallmark of the family line for generations. Another discovers a musical talent, which, when cultivated will bring joy to both the player and hearers alike.

Unfortunately, part of every person's inheritance is a sinful nature. John 3:6 states, *"That which is born of the flesh is flesh; and that which is born of the Spirit is spirit."* An earthly inheritance gives us a physical body and an active soul. Man's spiritual inheritance is separation from God's life and indwelling Presence. David cried, *"Behold, I was brought forth in iniquity, and in sin my mother conceived me"* (Psalm 51:5).

Until a man meets Jesus Christ and experiences a new birth of a spiritual dimension, his life is void of God's life and is swayed by a will that is sin controlled, self-motivated and satanically harassed. Sin gives a place to Satan. When people give themselves to carnal or fleshly activities, that is, actions that are contrary to the laws and principles of God, evil spirits find legal entrance to bind and afflict.

When man sinned in the beginning he came under a curse. So also did Satan. *"And the Lord God said to the serpent, 'Because you have done this, cursed are you more than all cattle, and more than every beast of the field; on your belly shall you go, and dust shall you eat all the days of your life'"* (Genesis 3:14).

Do serpents eat dust to sustain life? No, but a variety of rodents and other creatures. The serpent's food (Satan's food), was to be the flesh of man. Genesis 2:7 says that .... *"the Lord God formed man of dust from the ground"* .... Genesis 3:19 says that man would return to the ground, ... *"For you are dust, and to dust you shall return."*

What are we endeavouring to say? Every man or woman without Christ, walks according to the desires of his own self or flesh. By taking such a course, man attracts demonic activity into his life, just as metals are drawn to a magnet. Very often he becomes a seedbed for evil thoughts, which in turn spawn evil deeds, that bring him into the bondage of Satan.

In this state of separation from God, procreation takes place. While forming in the womb, a child is affected by the life-style of both father and mother. Spirits afflicting the parents seek entrance to the growing child and some measure of transference takes place even before birth. These afflictions may be physical, mental, emotional or spiritual. A non-Christian parent can do little or nothing to hinder such a transference of spirits.

In a later chapter we will consider the protection Christian parents can give a child being formed in the womb.

If the father or mother is a fearful person, spirits of fear will already have attached themselves to the child in the womb, and will seek to strengthen their hold as the child grows up. Such inherited bondages are as varied as the sins of men. Adulterers can pass on unclean sexual spirits. Alcoholics can pass on spirits of bondage to drink. Rejected people transfer spirits of rejection. A former generation affects the present one, the present generation affects the one to come. This continuance of satanic activity can only be broken by the intervention of Jesus Christ.

Although I opened myself to spirits of fear through various traumatic experiences, I am only too well aware that fear first was established in my life from my mother's womb. My dear mother was plagued by fear all her life. She was so anxious, so full of worry, so swayed by a variety of fears. From my earliest days the powers that gripped my mother began to influence and grip me. With this present understanding, I in no way condemn or blame my mother for what she passed on to me. She herself lived in much torment, not through her own desire, but by the desire of the tyrannical enemy. If only she had met Jesus as Deliverer, my childhood would have been so different. But can't we all say this? Rarely do parents, even Christian parents, understand the extent of the subversive activities of Satan. Because of our ignorance we offer no resistance, and evil spirits continue their works of destruction.

Sins of the Fathers

Like father, like son, goes the saying. How true this often is, and challenges us all to set a godly example for our children to imitate. In Exodus 34:6,7 we read of God revealing Himself to Moses:

Then the Lord passed by in front of him and proclaimed, "The Lord, the Lord God, compassionate and gracious, slow to anger, and abounding in lovingkindness and truth; who keeps lovingkindness

*for thousands, who forgives iniquity, transgression
and sin; yet He will by no means leave the guilty
unpunished, visiting the iniquity of fathers on the
children and on the grandchildren to the third and
fourth generations.''*

Again, a similar statement is made in Jeremiah
32:17—19:

*Ah Lord God! Behold, Thou hast made the heavens
and the earth by Thy great power and by Thine
outstretched arm! Nothing is too difficult for Thee,
who showest lovingkindness to thousands, but repayest the iniquity of fathers into the bosom of their
children after them, O great and mighty God. The
Lord of hosts is His name;
great in counsel and mighty in deed, whose eyes are
open to all the ways of the sons of men, giving to
everyone according to his ways and according to the
fruit of his deeds.*

…. *''But repayest the iniquity of the fathers into the
bosom of their children after them''* …. None of us live
unto ourselves. Our life-style, positive or negative, affects others, particularly our children. The Bible says
the sins of the fathers (and mothers — Psalm 109:
14—20), affect not only their children, but also their
grandchildren and great grandchildren. What a responsibility is ours as parents, to live godly lives so that we
pass on blessings to our seed and not curses.

There is a time to confess the sins of our fathers
unto God. Our fathers (and mothers) may be alive or
dead and our confession does not forgive their sins. Nor
are we responsible for their sins as such, but we have
been affected to some degree by their sins, whether we

38

know it or not, and by the demonic activity associated with those sins.

Hear the cry of Lamentations 5:7,8. *"Our fathers sinned, and are no more; it is we who have borne their iniquities. Slaves rule over us; there is no one to deliver us from their hand."*

In Leviticus 26 the Lord speaks of affliction being experienced because of the peoples' iniquities and the iniquities of their forefathers (verse 39). He then says that, *"If they confess their iniquity and the iniquity of their forefathers, in their unfaithfulness which they committed against Me, and also in their acting with hostility against Me"* (verse 40), that He would remember His covenant with their forefathers. ....*"I will remember for them the covenant with their ancestors, whom I brought out of the land of Egypt in the sight of the nations, that I might be their God. I am the Lord"* (verse 45).

These references refer to a people called by God. You may not have a Christian heritage, but the same principles apply. If people are afflicted who have had godly forebears, how much more the affliction of those with no godliness in the ancestry.

The Sin of Cannibalism

A missionary friend from Papua New Guinea described a dilemma facing the people amongst whom he laboured. Many fine young men and women were turning to Christ, being filled with the Holy Spirit, and being delivered from demonic bondages. Despite such movings of God, some were having great struggles to maintain a walk of victory. As he sought God for light, he was made aware of the effects of the "sins of the fathers". These new Christians had come out of a heritage of cannibalism. Some of their own fathers had eaten human flesh not so many years before. These barbaric acts surely must be some of the lowest fallen men could carry out. With new understanding, he encouraged these believers, to "confess the sins of their fathers", to confess the sins of cannibalism and to renounce every demonic bondage afflicting their own lives because of such shameful deeds. With this confession of sins came a dimension of liberty and victory never before experienced in the lives of those formerly struggling.

There is a transference from the womb. There is a transference from generation to generation. Spirits of fear are passed on through the Adamic inheritance, but there is power to break inherited bondages through the blood of Jesus Christ. *"Knowing that you were not redeemed with perishable things like silver or gold from your futile way of life inherited from your forefathers, but with precious blood, as of a lamb unblemished and spotless, the blood of Christ."* (1 Peter 1:18,19).

4. Through Traumas

Further breachings by spirits of fear into the human mind, emotions and will, occur in situations where a person experiences shock, stress and trauma. Recently we prayed for a fine teenager who had matured beyond her years through a four year crisis in which her mother finally died of cancer. To watch her mother be robbed of health, and finally of life, by spirits of infirmity, made a deep impression on this young woman. Spirits of sorrow had overwhelmed her and the fear of cancer was gripping her. As we ministered deliverance in Jesus' Name, she was wonderfully released from both the sorrows and the fears, and was set free to be able to enjoy her youth in a way she had not been able to before.

On another occasion we ministered to a woman who was intensely fearful that she had committed the unpardonable sin and had lost her salvation. Only as spirits of fear and condemnation were broken, could she truly realise that God was both with her and for her. During our ministry to her, the Lord revealed she was bound by spirits of the fear of death. The Spirit of God first showed me the bondage area and then put upon the screen of my mind a scene of a child looking into a coffin. When I shared the fear I discerned and the circumstances of its entrance, she readily remembered the occasion, when, as a child, she had to place some flowers on a coffin during a funeral. Her emotions could not handle this trauma and spirits of the fear of death found an opportunity to bind her. How clearly she remembered that day when that particular fear first found a place in her life. This fear linked in with her fear of losing her salvation. With no assurance of eternal life, the fear of death had mocked her until she became aware of the source of her plight and was set free.

As yet I have not settled the issue for myself of whether or not the body of a loved one should be viewed during a funeral service as is the Canadian custom. This

41

is not the custom in New Zealand or Australia from where we have come. It was at the age of twenty four years that I first viewed a dead body, and that was not at a funeral service but at the scene of an accident. The young man killed had attended evangelistic meetings we had been involved with just days beforehand, but had left rejecting the Gospel and its claims. Now it was too late to trust Christ. He had gone out into eternity unprepared, as far was we were aware.

In many places it is customary to pay last respects by viewing the open coffin, but for some, especially young children, this can be most traumatic, particularly if the person was a close relative or friend. I consider it unwise to subject children to this kind of an experience because evil spirits have no sense of "fairness" and can gain entrance easily through such traumas.

Many of you are aware of some past traumatic situation in which fear gained entrance to your life. Be assured that there is a way of escape and that you can live in a glorious freedom from every kind of fear.

5. Through Fearful Environments

We have seen that a traumatic experience can be the point at which spirits of fear gain entrance into a person's psyche. Spirits of fear also enter lives by what we could call the "absorption process".

We are like sponges, particularly as young children, and absorb a great variety of stimuli from our environment. Our homes and our families are important sources of both positive and negative influences. If our father was an angry man with regular outbursts of anger and violence towards a wife or children, we develop a fear of that anger, a fear of violence. If we are constantly being told we will never amount to anything, (this is a common occurrence in many homes) we develop a sense of failure and give entrance to a fear of failure. Over a period of time, we not only absorb words and attitudes, but also give place for spirits of failure and of the fear of failure to take up residence in our being.

A fear of insanity troubled me particularly during my late teen years. It was not a daily fear, but surfaced periodically to severely distress me. As an adult I was afraid of driving past mental institutions and even more afraid of visiting them. How did I become subject to this fear? I know only too well. My aunt, a nurse, was Matron of a hospital for many years. As a child I not only loved her because she was my aunt, and a very kind one at that, but I respected her as an expert. Wasn't she in charge of a hospital? Wasn't she skilled in understanding the physical and mental needs of people? With this admiration, I heard my aunt on many occasions over the years, tell my mother that if she continued living under the stresses she struggled with, that she would have a breakdown and end up in a mental asylum. In those days there was not the compassion expressed to the mentally ill as there is today. Those statements from "the one who knew" were absorbed into my life and gave entrance to a fear of insanity, firstly, in regard to my mother, and then later, in regard to myself.

To compound this fear, neighbours on either side of the family home made regular trips to mental hospitals.

They were the "strange ladies" next door. Would what happened to them happen to my mother too? How the enemy uses negative words and circumstances to lay a foundation for ongoing bondage and torment.

What sort of words fill your home? Are your children being influenced by words of peace and blessing or by words of tension and fear?

Chapter 5

Manifestations of Fear

The Newsweek article on Phobias stated, "Phobias can be triggered by virtually anything under the sun. They can be as common as acrophobia (fear of heights, from the Greek akros for heights or summits) or as relatively rare as trichophobia (fear of hair, from tricho for hair). The types that have been listed in medical literature number in hundreds and seem to be limited only by the ability of doctors to come up with the appropriate Greek or Latin names for them"*

So numerous are the types of fear that assail us, that volumes would have to be written to name them. Daily we are subject to feelings and emotions that are both positive and negative. Just to be anxious does not mean we are in bondage to spirits of anxiety (a type of fear), nor does going through a period of insecurity (also a type of fear), mean we are in demonic bondage to spirits of insecurity. Yet there are multitudes who are unduly gripped by anxiety, insecurity, inferiority, or worry. They are in bondage.

Some years ago I ministered to a man who had achieved a high level of success within his own nation as an athlete. He expressed that his drive to achieve

*© 1984, by Newsweek, Inc. All Rights Reserved. Reprinted by Permission.

was born of inferiority and embarrassment as a child, resulting from a particular physical affliction. His inner conflicts challenged him to set and pursue high goals as a young man. There is nothing wrong with achieving, or being the best we can in a field of endeavour, as long as we are not driven by negative motivating forces as he was.

Let us consider now some specific fears.

The Fear of Death

This is a very common affliction. Death holds apprehension and mystery. Most would rather not face this reality of even talk about it. Most parents raise their children to live but do not prepare them to die.

Hebrews 2:14,15 speaks of Christ: *"Since then the children share in flesh and blood, He himself likewise also partook of the same, that through death He might render powerless him who had the power of death, that is, the devil; and might deliver those who through fear of death were subject to slavery all their lives."*

Recently I prayed for a woman who opened herself to the fear of death some eight years previously when she entered hospital for major surgery for cancer. Since that operation the fear of death had gripped her, but not only that, also the fear of sickness, doctors, nurses and hospitals. Driving past the local hospital on her way to work was agony. How wonderfully Jesus released her that day.

The Fear of Sickness

Closely related to the fear of death is the fear of sickness. Sometimes this fear can be placed on people by well-meaning but unwise doctors. Also, as people read articles on diseases and the statistics associated with them, fear can gain a foothold unless we are on our guard. Often the fear of a particular sickness will eventually give place to the sickness itself.

A friend opened her heart to us some time ago. She was struggling with the fear of a certain disease, but her conflict was intensified because she felt that God had told her He wanted her to be crippled by this condition. Some time previously, as she was seeking God in prayer, a deceiving spirit injected thoughts into her mind, that she received as from the Lord. The spirits told her she would develop a certain disease which would ultimately place her in a wheel chair, but, said the spirits, in that condition she would be able to give herself to the ministry of intercession and so be much used of God.

Can you imagine her conflict? She desired to be used of the Lord and to do His will; yet she was afraid. Believing God had spoken, she read profusely about the disease, its symptoms, its stages, its conclusion. Unknowingly she was inviting the initial symptoms and the subsequent deterioration.

Shirley and I told her that God had not spoken to her, and went on to share the courageous struggle of a friend, who, by God's power and to the amazement of doctors, had overcome multiple sclerosis. Unknowingly we touched the very condition she felt she was to receive

47

"from God". We rebuked those deceiving spirits and spirits of fear in Jesus' Name, and before our eyes this woman was delivered of the fears and burdens that so cruelly oppressed her.

The Fear of Failure

Still fresh in my memory is the couple we prayed for, the husband being filled with inferiority and shyness (both spirits of fear), and the wife, with spirits of rejection and the fear of rejection. Common to both were strongholds built by spirits of failure and the fear of failure. He was so overwhelmed by a sense of failure that his release seemed to lift him from a great depth. Tears flowed freely as the Spirit of God encouraged him that the Lord was going to use him in His service.

The Fear of Rejection

All the fears listed so far are extremely common. Rejection and the fear of rejection are particularly rampant today, and we deal with them constantly.

We know a woman who is embarrassed about her parentage and appearance. (Embarrassment is a type of fear.) She is part negro and has a beautiful complexion and frizzy hair. Because she so rejects herself she is constantly straightening her hair so she will not appear to be negroid. Rejection, self-rejection and the fear of rejection are robbing her of rest and meaningful relationships with others. What a curse of the enemy.

The list of fears goes on: fear of people, disappointment, authority, embarrassment, rape, the supernatural, animals, enclosed spaces, open spaces, crowds, heights, flying, water, danger, fire, old age etc. One can be afraid of fear itself as was my experience. The Bible says in Proverbs 3:25: *"Do not be afraid of sudden fear, nor of the onslaught of the wicked when it comes."*

Recent trips away for us involved preaching in many churches and praying for people to be delivered. In one church, rather than sit up front on the platform I sat three rows back with Shirley and some friends. In front of us sat a young married woman who cried continuously. When it came time to pray for people after the preaching of the Word, she responded, accompanied by her husband and parents. They told me she was on tranquilizers, had had to leave her employment, and was in the midst of a break-down.

As we began to pray we came against the many different spirits that were overwhelming her. Suddenly I became aware that she had a fear of the Devil, a fact she readily agreed to. As we began to break this fear, I became aware that she also had a fear of God (not the necessary fear we earlier spoke of). To this also she readily agreed. She said she was a Christian, was frightened to pray, to come to church, to make any response to her heavenly Father. What a bondage, to fear God on one hand, and to fear Satan on the other. We continued to undo the chains that night to release her into the peace that passes all understanding.

Whatever the fear, God wants you to be free from it and to walk fear free.

Following are twenty five phobias classified with their medical names. For a fuller list, see the Appendix.

Acrophobia	fear of heights
Agoraphobia	fear of open spaces
Anthrophobia	fear of people
Autophobia	fear of being alone
Brontophobia	fear of thunder
Cancerophobia	fear of cancer
Claustrophobia	fear of enclosed spaces
Cynophobia	fear of dogs
Eisoptrophobia	fear of mirrors
Gamophobia	fear of marriage
Gephyrophobia	fear of crossing bridges
Hematophobia	fear of blood
Hydrophobia	fear of water
Kakorraphiaphobia	fear of failure
Logophobia	fear of words
Maniaphobia	fear of insanity
Nyctophobia	fear of darkness
Ochlophobia	fear of crowds
Peniaphoba	fear of poverty
Pyrophobia	fear of fire
Scopophobia	fear of being stared at
Tachophobia	fear of speed
Thanatophobia	fear of death
Xenophobia	fear of strangers
Zoophobia	fear of animals

Chapter 6

Building and Maintaining the Hedge

As wonderful as it is to break free from fear — in a later chapter we shall learn to do this — it is more wonderful to be kept from fear. A godly character and godly responses afford protection from all types of demonic inroads and the subsequent bondages, being in themselves a wall of protection. God desires our children to be formed free, born free, and to walk free. This is where a great responsibility lies with parents to build a hedge or wall of protection around their growing children, to maintain that wall of protection, and to teach their children to assume responsibility for the task as they grow in understanding and maturity.

What is a hedge? It is a barrier that keeps things in and keeps things out. It protects. It establishes boundaries. It provides security. Having lived in a wilderness environment, we know well the need for fences to keep cattle, horses and wildlife from trampling on our gardens.

In John 14:30 Jesus said, *"I will not speak much more with you, for the ruler of the world is coming, and he has nothing in Me."* What did He mean? Jesus was saying that there was a hedge of protection around His life and that Satan could find no place to penetrate it. There was no sin in Jesus Christ — no ground in Him where the enemy had any legal right of occupation. Death, the outworking of sin, was not at work in His life, yet He would die, because He had chosen to lay down His life with the purpose of taking it up again (John 10:17,18).

Let us turn to the Old Testament and learn some lessons from the life of Job.

Looking Behind the Scenes

Job was a man who was blameless, upright, fearing God and turning away from evil. Three times these same characteristics are mentioned within twenty-five verses of Scripture, characteristics that need to be part of our lives also if we are to stand strong against enemy infiltration. Satan knows when he has a legal right to gain entrance to bind. If we harbour unforgiveness, the welcome mat is out. If we neglect prayer, praise, the reading of the Word of God, our defences will soon be broken down. We are involved in daily spiritual warfare and a state of alert must be maintained at all times.

Even with a wall around us (the New Testament speaks of the armour of God, Ephesians 6:10—18), fiery darts will still come our way with the purpose of knocking us down and piercing the wall. The fact that an army is well equipped and well arrayed does not guarantee it will not come under attack. During such attacks we must stand firm and resist the enemy using the weapons of our spiritual warfare.

Spiritual Attack

A few years ago a couple we know well were ministering in Papua New Guinea. One day, as the husband was preaching, his wife saw a black arrow fly through the air and strike her husband in the chest. The arrow was not a material one and was seen only by his wife. At this time our friend was struck down with pneumonia. Returning to Australia, he was admitted to hospital, where complications set in that could have taken his life. Even though he recovered, doctors told him he would not be able to return to all aspects of his former lifestyle, which included regular rounds of golf. Though elderly, he embraced God's Word of healing, and slowly but surely returned to his former way of life. What started as an enemy attack could have ended tragically, had these servants of God not known the power of God's Word and its ability to defeat the enemy.

Job was a man blessed of God, as Job Chapter One tells us. Not only was he blessed with sheep, camels, oxen and servants, but he enjoyed the blessing of seven sons and three daughters.

As a concerned father he prayed regularly for his children and after times of festivity offered burnt offerings to God for he said, ..."*Perhaps my sons have sinned and cursed God in their hearts*" (Job 1:5).

Our look behind the scenes in Job's life commences from verse six where we read of Satan coming before the Throne of God. When the Lord asked Satan where he came from, Satan answered, ..."*From roaming about on the earth and walking around on it*" (verse

7). 1 Peter 5:8 says, *"Be of sober spirit, be on the alert. Your adversary, the devil, prowls about like a roaring lion, seeking someone to devour."* (Greek, Katapino: to drink down, devour, drown, swallow up.)

The Lord then went on to commend his servant Job for He was so delighted with his walk before Him (verse 8). Satan then answered the Lord, *"Does Job fear God for nothing? Hast thou not made a hedge about him and his house and all that he has, on every side? Thou has blessed the work of his hands, and his possessions have increased in the land"* (verses 9,10). Satan was displeased. As much as he wanted to afflict Job and his family he was unable. Job's righteousness, and no doubt the righteousness of his family members who were a reflection of his training and upbringing, hindered the penetration of Satan's evil intents. He was frustrated. He couldn't get through. Why? Because of the hedge!

Satan then challenges God. *"But put forth Thy hand now and touch all that he has; he will surely curse Thee to Thy face"* (verse 11).

In His wisdom and for purposes we may not fully understand, God allowed Satan to pierce the hedge but placed limitations as to the extent of his affliction. ....*" 'Behold, all that he has is in your power, only do not put forth your hand on him'. So Satan departed from the presence of the Lord"* (verse 12).

In the midst of struggles against demonic forces, how good it is to know that God is Sovereign in our personal affairs and that the enemy can only work within limits set by God. This is not to give place to passivity on our part but it brings great encouragement.

Having glimpsed behind the scenes, we turn, as it were, to what now unfolds on the stage of time. In the following seven verses of the chapter we read of the following calamities.

Calamity 1 The Sabeans attacked, took the donkeys and oxen, and slew the servants.

Calamity 2 The fire of God fell from heaven consuming sheep and servants.

Calamity 3 The Chaldeans raided the camels and killed the servants.

Calamity 4 A great wind struck the house killing Job's sons and daughters.

These tragedies struck simultaneously. They were satanically perpetrated. Perhaps there could have been natural explanations for each calamity, however, the Bible shows us what was happening back stage, behind the scenes, so we know clearly this was the work of Satan.

How often God gets blamed for events that are satanically insitigated. Insurance companies talk about "acts of God", but how often have they actually been "acts of Satan"? Our enemy is a destroyer. Let us recognise this and put up the hedge.

Job's response to this stripping indicated the depths to which God had built into his life godly character and responses. He mourned — and worshipped; *"Through all this Job did not sin nor did he blame God"* (verse 22). What a man! How would we respond under such circumstances, I wonder?

A Second Salvo

Although Satan was delighted with the destruction he had wrought, he still was not satisfied. Again he came before God's Throne; again he indicated he was roaming around on the earth; again God commended His servant Job. God said of him, ..."*And still he holds fast his integrity, although you incited Me against him, to ruin him without cause*" (Job 2:3). Remember, we are glimpsing things behind the scenes. Satan responded, ..."*Skin for skin! Yes, all that a man has he will give for his life. However, put forth Thy hand, now, and touch his bone and his flesh; he will curse Thee to Thy face*" (verses 4,5).

Satan had gone to the limits of divine permission and was straining to go further. Again God gives him release. ...."*Behold, he is in your power, only spare his life,*" said the Lord (verse 6).

The next verse takes us into the realm of time and human realities again. "*Then Satan went out from the presence of the Lord, and smote Job with sore boils from the sole of his foot to the crown of his head*" (verse 7). Once again we could put forward a natural explanation as to why this and that, but the Bible plainly says — SATAN DID IT!

Before we move on from this story, let us be aware that after his great trial, the Lord restored the fortunes of Job and increased all that he had twofold. "*And the Lord blessed the latter days of Job more than his beginning, and he had 14,000 sheep, and 6,000 camels, and 1,000 yoke of oxen, and 1,000 female donkeys. And he had seven sons and three daughters*" (Job 42:12,13).

Is Your Hedge Down?

We have already considered spirits being transferred during the time of pregnancy and through emotional trauma. Some other occasions of entrance are through pursuing wilfully areas of sin; harbouring resentment and unforgiveness; involvement in the occult, whether seriously or in fun; and through dishonouring our parents.

Earlier today, I prayed for a young man to be set free from spirits of insanity and the fear of insanity. As I prayed, spirits that had plagued and tormented his mind for years manifested and left. Many of his mind problems were compounded by years of drug abuse which had further depreciated his will to resist any enemy onslaught. I was reminded of Isaiah 5:1—7, where the Lord spoke of His people Israel as a vineyard and Judah as His delightful plant. God had placed His people "on a fertile hill and placed a hedge of protection around them" expecting a harvest of good fruits. Because of their continuous rebellion the hand of the Lord's protection was lifted off them as verses five and six declare.

"So now let Me tell you what I am going to do to My vineyard:

I will remove its hedge and it will be consumed; I will break down its wall and it will become trampled ground.

And I will lay it waste; It will not be pruned or hoed, but briars and thorns will come up. I will also charge the clouds to rain no rain on it."

With the removing of the hedge, the vineyard became consumed, the soil trampled; briars and thorns grew up, and the vineyard was stricken by drought. We well understand these pictures in the natural realm, but do we appreciate the spiritual parallel? Because we break God's laws, we lose His protection and experience wasting destruction by demonic forces that bring barrenness and drought within our souls.

When do we Start Building?

Christian parents can learn to cooperate with God and build protecting walls for themselves and their children. Even before a child is conceived, parents should be acknowledging their dependency upon the Lord for the anticipated new life and seeking His blessing on their union and the fruit of the womb. As a child is forming, parents can acknowledge daily the Lord's goodness, and declare protection to the developing child in the Name of Jesus Christ.

If the parents are aware of bondages in their lives that have not been completely removed as yet, they can declare protection to their child from any transferences in the Name of Jesus. The mother can, during times of daily rest, bless her forming child by speaking words of love and acceptance and acknowledge the blessing and protection of God upon her child.

Luke Chapter One shows clearly how John the Baptist was blessed as he was being formed. The angel of the Lord told Zacharias that his son would be filled with the Holy Spirit while yet in his mother's womb (Luke 1:15). When Elizabeth heard the greeting of Mary her cousin while in her sixth month of pregnancy, her child leaped for joy in her womb. Simultaneously Elizabeth and John were filled with the Holy Spirit (Luke 1:39—45). Isn't that wonderful! What affected Elizabeth affected John. Her joy at Mary's presence brought a response of joy to the unborn child. Her filling of the Holy Spirit flowed over to fill her son as well. So often we are aware of negative transference but let us be those who transfer the positive.

The time of birth itself needs to be bathed in prayer, that as the new life enters an unfamiliar environment, God's protection will overshadow. As they grow, our children need to be loved by both words and actions that will establish security in their lives. They need firm, loving, and consistent discipline, as this enables the wall to be built up around them. Children who are allowed to embrace rebellion, stubbornness and resentment, open themselves to spirits in these areas that will trouble them now and later as adults.

As we train our children to respect us as parents, and we need to live lives worthy of their respect, the wall is maintained and strengthened.

The building of this invisible wall and its maintenance is a daily task that requires much vigilance. The results of being sluggish are clearly portrayed in Proverbs 24:30—34, and can be summed up by the word "poverty".

I passed by the field of the sluggard,
And by the vineyard of the man lacking sense;
And behold, it was completely overgrown with thistles,
Its surface was covered with nettles,

59

And its stone wall was broken down.
When I saw, I reflected upon it;
I looked, and received instruction.
"A little sleep, a little slumber,
A little folding of the hands to rest,"
Then your poverty will come as a robber,
And your want like an armed man.

Death Wish

During recent months of praying with people we have
become distressed to discover the number of children
who have wished they could die. It is understandable
why many an adult has a death wish because of the buf-
fetings by so many destructive forces, but not children!
Why would a seven year old not wish to live and not
wish to play, play, play? What excitement should fill
the lives of youngsters as they grow and explore the
world around them. Why the sorrow, the distress, the
desire for death? Because the hedge has been broken
down, or because of the failure of parents to build the
wall around their children. Even more destitute are the
many children who have no one to take a personal concern for their well-being.

Our adopted children Martin and Carrie came from
a background of alcoholism, neglect and desertion.
Fortunately, the foster parents who cared for them
before they joined our family were very fine Christians,
and had begun to build a wall where there had been
none. Just loving them and causing them to feel secure
was a major part of the building process. So many of
the things we do to build parts of the wall are "non-

spiritual'', if that is the correct term. From my own childhood I have many pleasant memories of aunts and uncles who took an interest in me. I grew up with a sense of belonging, not only in our immediate family but within a wider family as well. Experiencing that security is so necessary for us all.

However, spiritual activities are necessary to balance the natural, and the foster parents of our children drew them into their evening devotional times which included singing, praying and teaching of the Word through Bible stories. To this activity we have added the memorising of Scripture. Even at the ages of three and five, Martin and Carrie could quote from memory readily a number of Psalms, and delighted and challenged many a parent to graft the Word of God into the hearts of their own children.

Fascination with Fantasy

The spiritual conflict in which we are engaged is with an unseen enemy;. and yet more and more he is revealing himself to the sight and senses of man. The current fascination with space and the extraterrestrial and the creatures who presumably live and war in this realm has reached epidemic proportions.

Arcades and game parlours are big business. Hollywood grosses millions of dollars within days of releasing some of the major feature films. Horrible demonic-like creatures have become heroes, as things, once considered ugly and repulsive, are embraced and considered beautiful. What is happening? The walls are down. The hedges are broken. Our children and youth have been invaded by demonic hordes and a generation is being prepared to embrace an even greater onslaught of the satanic. Indeed, the world is being prepared to greet and worship "the beast" of Revelation with all his lying signs and wonders.

Recently, I stayed in a Christian home and slept in the room of one of the boys. Peering down upon me was a large poster depicting some hairy hero from outer space that was nothing other than a demon form. How lax and blinded we are as Christians when we make room for such demonic activity! With every game that takes our time, with every poster or replica that fascinates us is released a measure of demonic activity. If you want to know further what some demons look like, simply look at the covers of many Rock albums available today. Demons are coming out of hiding, and, even though they are exposing themselves, few people seem alarmed.

Christian parents, please protect your children. Teach them. Train them. Impart to them the things of the Kingdom of God which is the realm of Light.

Seek God as families and be caught up with the reality of the Lord Jesus. May our children be trained to choose and desire the things that pertain to life and godliness. Let us do our part to build and maintain the hedge around their lives. Philippians 4:8 says, *"Finally, brethren, whatever is true, whatever is honorable, whatever is right, whatever is pure, whatever is lovely, whatever is of good repute, if there is any excellence and if anything worthy of praise, let your mind dwell on these things."*

Dealing with the Destructive

Not only are we to teach our children positive values; we have a responsibility to keep out the negative. Therefore it is important to check the following points and see if adjustments or radical changes may need to be made. Wisdom is required, particularly with older children, in implementing guidelines where there has been a general laxity. Our children need to be working with us. They need to understand that restrictions are for their own benefit and therefore not to resist that which is for their good.

Television

Without a doubt, the viewing of television plays a major role in shaping the outlook on life and the personal morality of our children. Many view TV for forty hours a week and, although some programmes may have no detrimental effect on their lives, much of what is presented does. Cartoons are not harmless as some may think but many are of an occult nature; many are filled with violence; still others impart philosophies that are contrary to the truth of God. And yet, what are cartoons in the light of the insidious, pornographic, devil inspired adult programmes and videos that many children view?

Multitudes of children open themselves to demonic bondages of fear, sorrow, rebellion, violence, lust, etc., as they get caught up in programmes that their emotions are too fragile to handle, or by giving consent to ungodly attitudes and actions.

Having stayed in many Christian homes over a number of years, we are sometimes staggered to see the lack of concern by some parents as to what the children are viewing. That which is being taught by parents and church is being challenged and disparaged on the screen.

Television viewing in a Christian home needs to be regulated so that it can be a beneficial instrument rather than one of destruction. If it cannot be regulated, it is far better not to have a television in the home at all.

Literature

What sort of literature is in your home? What sort of books are the children reading? Recently, I picked up a book full of grotesque pictures, depicting scenes from some current movies. It was a children's book, and when I brought it to the attention of the parents, who were missionaries, they immediately burned it. It had been perused by children as yet unable to read but already keenly sensitive to images that cause fear to be implanted on their imaginations. Parents need to carefully select the books their younger children read and to guide the older children in their choice of reading materials. Young people should have a clear concept of what to accept and what to reject in the way of literature.

Music

Music is one of the most powerful forces regulating attitudes and behaviour in our world today. How masterfully Satan is using this medium to brainwash our present generation. Let us make use of this powerful means of influence and communication by having our homes filled with edifying Christian music that is Christ glorifying and based in the truth of God's Word. Let us teach our children to delight in music, Christian and secular, that is beneficial not harmful. Is the hedge around your child being pierced by the lyrics of songs that are detrimental to Christian character and growth?

Games

Many hours of family fun can be centred around a variety of games. Surely never before has a selection of blatantly demonic games such as Dungeons and Dragons been readily available. To participate in such games is to open oneself to demonic influence and to schooling in the ways of the occult. Even video games need to be selected with caution. It occurred to me recently that many such games have only to do with "destruction", and as youngsters give hours of mind and will to destroy, they are being programmed in Satan's train of thought, for he is The Destroyer (Revelation 9:11).

Let us be wise. Let us be builders and not destroyers and have family fun around games that are in no way detrimental.

Schooling

The move towards Christian schooling in recent years, indicates that God is concerned our children have an education based on His Word and not on the atheistic philosophies of humanism. It is time for all Christian parents to consider what is being taught in the schools their children attend and evaluate that input in the light of God's Word.

Home schooling with a Christian curriculum is an important alternative to secular education. Because we travel much we teach our own children in this way. Although it is time consuming, the results are extremely worthwhile. We know what is being sown into our children and can expect to reap a harvest of good things. Daily, through the schooling, we are building and maintaining the hedge.

Another area that parents can give children guidance in is the selection of companions with whom they will spend their spare time. It is impossible to keep our children entirely separate from an evil world, nor are we to be so separate from it that we have no influence upon our fellow man. It is our responsibility, however, to use wisely the privilege we have of moulding the lives of our children for the service of the King, and to do this we must be in control of the influences that will shape the nature and attitudes of our children.

Satan desires to curse; Jesus desires to bless. Both have eternity in view. Let us fulfil our responsibility as parents with wisdom. Let us purpose to work with God to build and maintain the hedges of protection.

Chapter 7

Christ the Deliverer

A deliverer is one who releases or rescues another from captivity, harm or corruption.

The Israelites posed a threat to the Egyptians because of their growing numbers in the land of Egypt, so Pharaoh ...."*appointed taskmasters over them to afflict them with hard labor*" .... (Exodus 1:11). Furthermore, the Egyptians .... "*made their lives bitter with hard labor in mortar and bricks and at all kinds of labor in the field, all their labors which they rigorously imposed on them*" (Verse 14).

Cries from these afflicted ones were spurned by men but heeded by God. While pasturing the flock of Jethro, Moses was apprehended by God and commissioned to be the instrument through which His deliverance would be manifested. "*And the Lord said, 'I have surely seen the affliction of My people who are in Egypt, and have given heed to their cry because of their taskmasters, for I am aware of their sufferings. So I have come down to deliver them from the power of the Egyptians, and to bring them up from that land to a good and spacious land, to a land flowing with milk and honey'*" .... (Exodus 3:7,8).

For eighty years Moses had been in training for this

hour, forty years as the son of Pharaoh's daughter, and forty years shepherding in the wilderness. God called Moses to deliver the people, and yet it was to be by God's hand through His servant that deliverance would come. What an exciting account Exodus presents, as, with supernatural authority and by signs and wonders, Moses leads the people out of slavery. Moses was a deliverer. He rescued the people out of captivity and harm.

It is important to note that things got worse before they got better for the Israelites. Even when Moses, their deliverer, arrived on the scene and spoke God's Word to Pharaoh, release came only after further affliction. Exodus 5 informs us of increased burdens placed upon the Israelites. The Egyptians were most reluctant to let their prey go. It was only by a strong hand that full deliverance would come. This is often the experience of people today as well. When the word of release is spoken, demonic powers "dig in their toes" so to speak, and will only leave the afflicted after persistant confrontations in the Name of the Lord.

How many are the deliverers in Bible history. We all know of David, of Gideon, of Samson, and so on, but none were as mighty as God's Son, Jesus Christ, who was sent by the Father to be The Deliverer, not of one nation, but of all nations; not of a few, but of many.

1. Deliverance Through His Earthly Ministry

As Jesus commenced His public ministry He went forth to preach, teach, deliver and heal. He entered His home

synagogue and quoted the words of the prophet Isaiah
from Isaiah 61:

The Spirit of the Lord is upon Me,
Because He anointed Me to preach the gospel to the
poor.
He has sent Me to proclaim release to the captives,
And recovery of sight to the blind,
To set free those who are downtrodden,
To proclaim the favorable year of the Lord.

Luke 4:18,19

It is estimated that Jesus spent up to one third of His
public ministry in casting out demons and healing the
sick. Jesus was the greatest of all deliverers. HE IS THE
DELIVERER. He walked through time unruffled by the
circumstances that so often cause us to panic. No situation was beyond His ability to change.

Deliverance from sin

Multitudes flocked to see Him, to hear Him, and to be
touched by His hands. People recognised Him as the
long promised Messiah and quickly the news spread
abroad of the miracles He was performing.

On one occasion when Jesus was teaching in a house,
a paralytic man was carried by four men to where He
was. As they saw the large crowd, they realised it was
not possible to penetrate it. Ascending to the roof, they
dug an opening and lowered their cargo to the room
below.

Looking upon the helpless man, Jesus saw beyond
the physical need to that of his soul. This man was not
right with God. His sins had not been forgiven. He was

not ready to face eternity. Sensing the cry of the man and responding to the faith being released, Jesus said, …. *"My son, your sins are forgiven"* (Mark 2:5). With that, an inner release took place, and the burden of unforgiven sin that yokes all who do not know Christ as Lord and Saviour, lifted from him. Jesus delivered him from his sins. This is the greatest deliverance anyone can experience because it relates to our relationship with God and to our eternal destiny. As great as the need for healing of the affliction of the body and soul may be, the need for forgiveness of sins is always greater. After Jesus had taken care of the paralytic's spiritual need, however, he also healed him physically.

Deliverance from self

Because of Adam's fall, man inherited a nature that is sin-prone and sin-saturated. As great as it is to be delivered from our sins, God wants to deliver us from the power of sin that causes us to sin. Only as we abandon our lives to Christ's Lordship can we be released from the sin principle at work in our lives. Jesus wants to deliver us from ourselves.

Romans chapter 8:1,2 says, *"There is therefore now no condemnation for those who are in Christ Jesus. For the law of the Spirit of life in Christ Jesus has set you free from the law of sin and death."*

A rich ruler approached Jesus one day expressing his desire to obtain eternal life. Jesus stressed the importance of keeping God's Law and quoted five of the Ten Commandments to him. The ruler responded by saying that from his youth up he had kept the commandments. Despite such a confession, Jesus looked into his heart and saw that his life was motivated and dominated by the love of money. Only as this area was surrendered to Christ's Lordship could this man be truly delivered from himself and therefore Jesus responded with this pertinent directive: ...."*One thing you still lack; sell all that you possess, and distribute it to the poor, and you shall have treasure in heaven; and come, follow Me*" (Luke 18:22).

The man's response was one of sadness. How could he give away his riches? How could he bless the poor? How could he focus on the eternal when he was so absorbed with the temporal? In the end, he turned away from Jesus, who had wanted to be the focal point of his life, to deliver him from slavery to himself, and to motivate him to serve others.

Newness of life

A baptismal service we experienced in Australia will live with me all my days. One of a number of new Christians we were baptising in a private swimming pool, was a visiting serviceman who, only recently, had become a Christian. At the pool-side and in the presence of his former wife and their children, now members of our church, he made a strange request: to be allowed to remain under water for awhile. So, for what seemed a long time to those gathered around this unusual sight, he remained under the water in a position of identification with death, praying to God and declaring the death of the old nature. His old ways were past, and he was identifying with Christ in a new life lived unto

71

God and no longer motivated by self-interest. Suddenly he burst from the water to the air as from the old life into the new. His baptism was no mere form, but the expression of a true change within. Jesus had delivered him from slavery to self, and, by faith, he was declaring newness of life through the resurrection of Jesus from the dead (Romans 6:1—11).

Deliverance from sickness and spirits

The message of deliverance from sin and self does not always attract an immediate response from people bent on going their own way. However the message of deliverance from sickness, disease, fear, and every other bondage of the Devil does draw the attention of the human ear, and provides a platform for declaring the message and claims of the Kingdom of God.

Acts 10:38 declares that God anointed Jesus of Nazareth with the Holy Spirit and with power and that He went about doing good and healing all who were oppressed by the Devil. How simply the Word declares that those needing healing were "under the dominion" of evil spirits.

And Jesus was going about in all Galilee, teaching in their synagogues, and proclaiming the gospel of the kingdom, and healing every kind of disease and every kind of sickness among the people.

And the news about Him went out into all Syria; and they brought to Him all who were ill, taken with various diseases and pains, demoniacs, epileptics, paralytics; and He healed them.

Matthew 4:23,24

He healed them, says the Scripture. The word "heal" is the Greak word therapeuo, from which we get the English "therapeutic". Therapeuo means "to serve as an attendant" and also "to care for, treat, cure, and heal the sick". The word "pains" is the Greek basanos, which means "torture" or "torment". How ably this covers the realm of fear. Fear tortures and torments both soul and body.

Alone in Luke 4 there are three accounts of His delivering ministry. While in the synagogue at Capernaum he cast an unclean spirit out of a man. Going to Peter's home he rebuked a high fever afflicting Peter's mother-in-law and it left her. In verses 40 and 41 we read:

And while the sun was setting, all who had any sick with various diseases brought them to Him; and laying His hands on every one of them, He was healing them.

And demons also were coming out of many, crying out and saying, "You are the Son of God!" And rebuking them, He would not allow them to speak, because they knew Him to be the Christ.

One can read about deliverance but there is nothing like experiencing it first hand. Until I met Jesus as Deliverer and Healer, I had suffered daily with life-long breathing difficulties. When the spirits causing the affliction were confronted and cast out, healing automatically followed. It took two days for the congestion to clear, and I awoke that second morning to find myself breathing freely. Jesus heals today. He is the Great Deliverer.

In a Sunday evening service during a recent campaign

we shared on how we can take authority over afflictions in Jesus' Name. The following evening the church gathered for a barbecue at which an excited mother told us of the transformation that had taken place in her three year old son. For some months the parents had watched him being constantly tormented by fear, but were unable to help him. Encouraged by the previous evening's challenge, the parents had returned home and laid hands on their boy and told those spirits of fear to leave him. The change was sudden and obvious. They were delighted not only to see their son delivered, but also to realise that God had wrought this miracle through their active involvement.

2. Deliverance Through His Death and Resurrection

Throughout the duration of His earthly ministry Jesus delivered and healed, but the purpose of God in sending His Son to the earth was not to be restricted to one nation and one generation. The coming of Christ was to have worldwide repercussions affecting all peoples that were to follow. God has a world in mind. His purpose is that people from every tongue, every tribe and every nation on earth should make up His Church. *"For God so loved the world, that He gave His only begotten Son, that whoever believes in Him should not perish, but have eternal life"* (John 3:16). In later years, John wrote, ... *"The Son of God appeared for this purpose, that He might destroy the works of the devil"* (1 John 3:8). How did Jesus destroy the works of Satan? By being crucified and offering Himself unto the Father as a sinless, substitutionary sacrifice. By receiving the punishment we deserved through our breaking of God's Law. By bearing away our sins and releasing us from judgment.

It was His death and resurrection from the dead that broke forever Satan's legal right to hold man in captivity. Colossians 2:15 states that Christ disarmed the rulers and authorities (satanic principalities), and made a public display of them, triumphing over them through His cross.

Understanding the work of the Cross is crucial to our walking in victory. Divine justice was fully satisfied in this ultimate sacrifice. The Old Testament saints offered their sacrifices looking ahead to the "perfect sacrifice" yet to come. Blood from animals only covered their sins but could not remove them. The blood of Jesus Christ, God's Lamb, pictured through the countless animal sacrifices over the centuries, alone could atone for sin (Hebrews 9).

We look back and see the Cross as an historic event that forever changed the history of the world. Before the Cross believers looked ahead. Whether people looked into the future, or whether they look back into the past, it is the Cross that commands our attention.

Satan knows the power of the Cross, but do we? How he opposes the preaching of the Gospel. He hates the proclamation of his eternal defeat through the blood of Christ.

Revelation 12:11 speaks of believers overcoming Satan ...."*because of the blood of the Lamb and because of the word of their testimony*" .... We are to declare boldly to spirits of fear and every kind of affliction that their right to hold us in captivity is over. A confession of what the Word of God says the blood of Jesus has accomplished for us needs to be upon our lips constantly. This declation is one of the greatest weapons of our warfare. Our weapons are launched through our mouth and are .... *"divinely powerful for the destruction of fortresses"* (2 Corinthians 10:4).

Paul declared, ... *"we preach Christ crucified, to the Jews a stumbling block, and to Gentiles foolishness, but to those who are the called, both Jews and Greeks, Christ the power of God and the wisdom of God"* (1 Corinthians 1:23,24).

A few verses later he declared, *"For I determined to know nothing among you except Jesus Christ, and Him crucified"* (2 Corinthians 2:2).

Satan has been defeated and dethroned by the death and resurrection of Christ.

3. Deliverance Through His Church

Limited to His earthly body, Jesus ministered in one location at one time, but through His Body, the Church, the Lord is able to reach out and touch lives wherever His people are located. Even during His earthly ministry, the Lord multiplied His effectiveness by sending out those who were His disciples.

"And having summoned His twelve disciples, He gave them authority over unclean spirits, to cast them out, and to heal every kind of disease and every kind of sickness.

These twelve Jesus sent out after instructing them" ....

Matthew 10:1,5

"Now after this the Lord appointed seventy others, and sent them two and two ahead of Him to every city and place where He Himself was going to come. And the seventy returned with joy, saying, 'Lord, even the demons are subject to us in Your Name.'"

Luke 10:1,17

Having risen from the dead He appeared to His disciples and commissioned them to go into all the world and preach the gospel to all creation (Mark 16:15).

"And these signs will accompany those who have believed: in My name they will cast out demons, they will speak with new tongues;

they will pick up serpents, and if they drink any deadly poison, it shall not hurt them; they will lay hands on the sick, and they will recover."

So then, when the Lord Jesus had spoken to them, He was received up into heaven, and sat down at the right hand of God.

And they went out and preached everywhere, while the Lord worked with them, and confirmed the word by the signs that followed.

Mark 16:17—20

Signs point the way. Signs give needed information. The four signs here mentioned that followed the preaching of the Word point the way to Christ as Saviour and Lord. They provide the information that Christ has risen. These signs follow believers — those who exercise faith in God's Word.

1. Supernatural Authority

...."*in My name they will cast out demons*" *....*

The authority to deal with the realm of the demonic is the first in the listing of *"signs (that) accompany those who have believed"* . It also receives the first mention in the previous commissions of Jesus. Yet, in our day, it is the last thing most Christians consider doing. No wonder there are so many bondages amongst the people of God. *"Behold, I have given you authority to tread upon serpents and scorpions, and over all the power of the enemy, and nothing shall injure you"* (Luke 10:19).

2. Supernatural Tongues

...."*they will speak with new tongues*" *....*

Speaking in tongues or languages one has never learned are signs of the Holy Spirit being poured out. Jesus Himself is the Baptiser in the Holy Spirit (Luke 3:16). On the day of Pentecost as the disciples were filled with the Spirit they *....*"*began to speak with other tongues as the Spirit was giving them utterance"* (Acts 2:4). Amazement filled the hearts of people from many lands as they heard them in their own languages speaking of the mighty deeds of God (Acts 2:11).

As people repent and believe in Jesus Christ, it is God's intention that they become filled with the Holy Spirit and experience the power of God, enabling them to continue in their Christian walk. One of the benefits of being filled with the Spirit is to speak in tongues, to experience the releasing of our human spirit in direct communication with the Father (1 Corinthians 14:2).

Speaking in Maori

A few months ago we were ministering in our native
New Zealand. During a time of praying for people after
a meeting, I had an experience which expanded my
understanding of speaking in tongues.

The congregation was made up of predominately
Maori people and as I prayed for a particular woman,
a spirit reacted in her and resisted my commands to
leave her in Jesus' Name. This made me more aggressive and I began to speak (command) in tongues, as
is often my practice. Suddenly the woman exclaimed
that I was speaking in the Maori language. I assured
her that I could not speak in Maori. When I asked her
what I was saying, she insisted that I knew what I was
saying. In fact, I didn't, although I knew I was address-
ing the spirits binding her. When she finally realised
this was a "sign" following the preaching of the Word,
she told me what was being said. Every so often
during the hour of praying for her, I would stop and
ask what the Spirit of God was saying. It was a most
awesome experience. What really impressed me was
that I was speaking in the Spirit, and trampling upon
demons. Immediately Luke 10:19 came to mind where
Jesus said to His disciples that He had given them
authority to ...."*tread upon serpents and scorpions and
over all the power of the enemy*" .... This experience
has expanded by prayer vocabulary when I pray with
my understanding. I say to spirits, "In Jesus' Name
I trample upon you, I crush you, I destroy your inroads

79

in this life''.

During this time, the pastor's wife who was working with me, was ministering in the word of knowledge and discernings of spirits in a remarkable way. The Lord revealed particular spirits and curses that had come into the woman's life through her Maori heritage. As I continued to speak in Maori, I noticed the tone of my voice changing and was aware that the Lord was now speaking a word directly to the lady herself. Being curious, I stopped to ask what the Lord was saying. He was speaking words of edification and encouragement.

Moving to others, I began to pray over them in both English and Maori. At 1.00am I finally left the church and travelled with a Maori man to his home in the country. As we drove, he commented on the fact that I had prayed over his ten year old foster daughter in Maori. When I asked him what I had been saying as I was casting demons out of her, he said, ''You were trampling upon the demons''. Hallelujah! It also encouraged me to know that the way the Holy Spirit had taught me to come against demonic bondages speaking with my understanding, was the very way the Holy Spirit was Himself dealing with the enemy. To further emphasise the awe of that evening, I discovered the next day that I had been speaking in the Maori dialect of the Ngati Tu Wharetoa people, the very dialect spoken in the district in which we were ministering.

Speaking in Spanish

These experiences have increased our faith to believe for further such manifestations. Only a month ago, as we ministered to a person from Costa Rica, Shirley began to minister a beautiful word of encouragement in the Spanish tongue without any knowledge of Spanish whatsoever. Oh for more signs to confirm the preaching of the Word.

3. Supernatural Protection

....*"they will pick up serpents, and if they drink any deadly poison, it shall not hurt them"* ....

How powerfully this was experienced by Paul after being shipwrecked on the island of Malta. When a viper fastened to him, the local people expected him to fall down dead, but God supernaturally protected His servant. This proved to be a convincing sign to prepare the people to receive his ministry in their midst.

A missionary friend of ours, has, on two occasions, been bitten by scorpions that could have seriously affected him. On both occasions he experienced no ill effects which proved a powerful witness to the native people.

4. Supernatural Power

....*"they will lay hands on the sick and they will recover"* ....

It is God's will to heal. Jesus healed all who came to Him (Matthew 8:16,17; Luke 4:40,41), and has purposed that His healing virtue should continue to flow through His Church today. The gifts of the Holy Spirit include gifts of healings and workings of miracles (1 Corinthians 12:9,10).

Two weeks ago I witnessed an evangelist praying for the deaf. Many deaf ears were opened that night, but particularly noteworthy was the healing of a young boy. Deaf and dumb from birth, he was prayed for, and, the deaf spirits being cast out, he began to hear for the first time ever. A short time later, he responded to teaching and began to speak as well. Tears came to my eyes as the compassion of Christ was manifested in this act of deliverance. Jesus heals today and is the same yesterday, today, and forever (Hebrews 13:8). He heals through His Church today.

Now that we know Jesus Christ is The Deliverer from sin, self, sickness and spirits, ''How,'' we ask, ''do we break free from fear?''

Firstly:	Acknowledge your need of deliverance from fear.
Secondly:	Acknowledge you are bound by spirits of fear.
Thirdly:	Yield to Jesus Christ as Lord and Saviour.
Fourthly:	Look to Jesus Christ as The Deliverer.

Chapter 8

Speaking to the Mountain

God wants you to be a mountain mover. A mountain is not only a natural upward projection of the earth's surface but can also be defined figuratively, as anything of great quantity or size. Fear may seem as firmly established as a mountain in your life, but God wants you to remove it.

That God wants you to be involved may sound contradictory, since we have just gone to some length to acknowledge Jesus Christ as The Deliverer. This however, is not so. We must learn to cooperate with God to bring deliverance to pass in our lives. When Jesus commissioned His disciples to go into all the world, we learn that *"they went out and preached everywhere, while the Lord worked with them, and confirmed the Word by the signs that followed"* (Mark 16:20). It was not the Lord alone heralding the Word, nor was it man alone, but God and man working together. As men spoke the Word, the Lord Jesus, by His Spirit, bore witness to the truth and produced signs and wonders to confirm it.

John the Baptist was a mountain mover. As he preached a baptism of repentance for forgiveness of sins, and as people responded to his words, mountains or obstacles in the lives of people were removed, preparing a people to receive the Messiah and the message He would soon bring (Isaiah 40:3—5; Luke 3:4—6).

In 1 Corinthians 13:2 we read of faith and love being linked together in the removing of mountains .... *"and if I have all faith so as to remove mountains, but do not have love, I am nothing."* Obviously, faith is the key to removing mountains, and it is God's desire that mountain movers not only know His power but are also motivated by His love.

Healing the Epileptic

On one occasion the disciples of Jesus were trying to bring deliverance to a boy who had been brought to them by his father. Over the years the spirits in the boy had thrown him into convulsions and had tried to destroy him by throwing him into fires or had tried to drown him in water. The disciples had known great success in delivering people from all sorts of afflictions, no doubt including the affliction with which they were now faced, but this time they seemed powerless to help.

After Jesus set the boy free, the disciples asked Him why they had not been able to do what He had just done. He responded by saying .... *"Because of the littleness of your faith; for truly I say to you, if you have faith as a mustard seed, you shall say to this mountain, 'Move from here to there,' and it shall move; and nothing shall be impossible to you. But this kind does not go out except by prayer and fasting"* (Matthew 17:20,21). It wasn't that the disciples had no faith, but they lacked the sufficiency of faith needed to break the strength of this demonic stronghold. Obviously prayer and fasting was the key to releasing a greater level of faith and hence experience a greater dimension of God's power.

Jesus referred to the epilepsy as a mountain that needed to be spoken to. .... *"you shall say to this mountain, 'Move from here to there,' and it shall move"* ....(verse 20).

As Jesus spoke to mountains of affliction, so we are to speak to them in His Name. Even in the natural, our words have far-reaching consequences. They can ensnare us or release us. Constant negative words give place to demonic activity that works against us; positive words (words harmonising with Scriptural truth), release the moving of the Spirit of God on our behalf. What we speak in the natural is temporal and passes away. The words we speak in the Name of Jesus have the authority of the conquering Christ behind them, and these are the words that will move mountains. Everywhere Jesus went, He spoke words. He is the Father's example to us of how we should walk, act, and speak. When we learn to speak as He did, we will indeed move mountains.

Jesus Forgave Sins by His Words

Mark 2 recounts the story previously referred to, of the healing of a paralytic man. As he was borne by friends on a pallet to where Jesus was, they discovered an enthralled crowd, for .... *"He was speaking the word to them."* When Jesus "saw" the inward need of the paralysed man, a need far greater than his physical affliction, and when He "saw" their faith being

85

expressed through the determined efforts to be in His presence, Jesus spoke to the paralytic and said .... *"My son your sins are forgiven"* (verse 5).

The scribes immediately reacted with criticism, because they knew only God could forgive sins and did not acknowledge Jesus as the Son of God. In order to show them His authority to forgive sins, He spoke to the paralytic, *"I say to you, rise, take up your bed and go home"* (verse 11). Two miracles were performed that day: one seen, one unseen.

The unseen was that of the cleansing of his soul from the effects of sin. The seen was evident to all: a man no longer immobilised, but one whose physical responses were normal. How did these miracles come about? Through words.

Jesus has commissioned His Church to preach the Gospel and to forgive or retain the sins of people. *"If you forgive the sins of any, their sins have been forgiven them; if you retain the sins of any, they have been retained"* (John 20:23). How is this done? By words.

Jesus Cast Out Demons by His Words

Time and time again Jesus used His authority and released the power of the Kingdom of God to drive out demons by words. Matthew 8:16 simply says, *"He cast out the spirits with a word"*. The healing of the epileptic boy, previously mentioned, was wrought through words. *"And Jesus rebuked him (the demon), and the demon came out of him, and the boy was cured at once"* (Matthew 17:18). An epileptic boy delivered by words.

While teaching in the Capernaum synagogue an

unclean spirit cried out through Jewish lips. ...."*What do we have to do with You, Jesus of Nazareth? Have You come to destroy us? I know who You are — the Holy One of God!*" (Mark 1:24). Jesus rebuked the spirit, saying ...."*Be quiet, and come out of him!*" *And throwing him into convulsions, the unclean spirit cried out with a loud voice, and came out of him* (Mark 1:25,26).

Jesus has commissioned His Church to preach the Gospel and to cast out demons. As He sent out His disciples He gave them authority to exercise in two distinct areas. Matthew 10:1 says, "*And having summoned His twelve disciples, He gave them authority over unclean spirits, to cast them out, and to heal every kind of disease and every kind of sickness.*"

These orders have never been withdrawn. After rising from the dead, He commissioned disciples for generations with the orders He had so clearly received from His Father. ...."*Go into all the world and preach the Gospel to all creation*" (Mark 16:15). The first sign to accompany believers was to be the casting out of demons! "*And these signs will accompany those who have believed: in My Name they will cast out demons*" ....(verse 17). Again it is the responsibility of the believer to accomplish this by words.

Jesus Healed the Sick by His Words

A leper came to Jesus and earnestly cried out to be made whole, should the Lord be willing to heal him. Jesus, moved with compassion, stretched out His hand and touched him. ...."*I am willing; be cleansed*" (Mark

87

1:41). With this spoken declaration he was made whole. Jesus healed by His words.

Entering Capernaum a centurion came to Him declaring that his servant was lying paralysed and suffering great pain. (Literally, fearfully tormented). When Jesus said he would come and heal him, the centurion responded, saying, ... *"Lord, I am not qualified for You to come under my roof, but just say the word (literally — say with a word), and my servant will be healed"* (Matthew 8:8). The centurion then explained that he recognised the authority that Jesus had. Jesus marvelled at the faith expressed by this Gentile and simply said, ..."*Go your way; let it be done to you as you have believed"* (Matthew 8:13). The moment Jesus spoke, the servant, although absent from the sound of Jesus' words, was healed.

Jesus has commissioned His Church to preach the Gospel and heal the sick. How is it done? By words.

Jesus raised the Dead by His Words

How powerless is mortal man when he faces the inevitability of death. While there is life there is hope, goes the saying, but when there is no life there is no hope — usually. Jairus, a synagogue ruler, sought out Jesus in order that He might raise up his young daughter who was at the point of death. The grief stricken father quickly led Jesus toward his home, but even before reaching it the word came that his daughter had died. Jesus, also hearing the message, urged Jairus not to be afraid but to believe. Seeing the mourners already weeping and wailing loudly, Jesus took the child's father and mother, as well as His own companions, and entered the room where the girl lay. What did Jesus do? He took the child by the hand and spoke, ... *"Little girl, I say to you arise!"* (Mark 5:41). Upon that declaration a miracle occurred. Her soul rejoined her body and the power of God quickened and restored her body and she immediately arose, and a little later was eating once again. How was she raised? By words.

Jesus has commissioned His Church to preach the Gospel and to raise the dead (Matthew 10.8). How is it done? By words.

The Importance of Faith

For many years I sought to be changed by God's power. I prayed earnestly and fasted regularly for freedom from fears and other bondages. When visiting servants of God came by, I sat under their ministries, hoping something would happen. Often I sought them out privately, hoping for the instant miracle that would be the answer to all my prayers. But nothing ever happened. No progress was ever made. I became increasingly disappointed because I did not know what else to do to touch God or be touched by Him. My life was summed up by one word: torment. Fear torments, and how the enemy troubled me even as a wholehearted servant of Christ.

Finally, the turning point came. For twelve months I had drawn aside to seek God without distraction, spending my days in prayer, fastings, and reading the Scriptures. The cry of years was intensified as I constantly called on God to work a miracle. "Lord you can do anything. You're a God of miracles. Please help me. Please set me free.'' What was I doing? Placing the initiative on God and telling Him He was responsible to bring the change. What a revelation it was to hear the voice of the Holy Spirit within, as I knelt one day in prayer. His voice came at a time of brokenness, when I was so depleted of strength that I did not feel I had enough energy to continue to seek God. What did the Holy Spirit say? ''I want you to rise up in resurrection life.'' What did I immediately say in response? ''But how Lord?'' Again the voice of God clearly spoke within me, speaking two distinct words. ''By faith.''

By faith! How these words were quickened to me and were to be a source of life and strength over the following weeks and months. After years of silence, God had personally spoken, and with His Word came faith. My attention was drawn to Mark 11 in particular, and through daily reading and meditating a doorway into a whole new dimension was opened before me.

In our book CHRISTIAN SET YOURSELF FREE one chapter, The Key of Faith, underscores the importance of faith in the life of a believer. The latter portion of this chapter, quoted below, explains how we can learn to take the initiative in bringing God into our experience.

Faith Relates to the Unseen

''Now faith is .... the conviction (AV: evidence) *of things not seen.''*

Hebrews 11:1

Evidence proves the existence of something. It is impossible to have evidence for something that does not exist. In spiritual things, faith is our evidence.

The natural eye does not see the kingdom of God with its vast resources made available to us through Calvary. Ephesians 1:3 says that God .... *"has blessed us with every spiritual blessing in the heavenly places in Christ."*

Just because we don't see this realm or see its provision, does not mean that it does not exist. In fact, the unseen realm is more real than the seen, in the sense that it is eternal. Our world had a beginning and will have an end. The unseen realm is eternal, and into this realm we reach by faith.

If I were to hold a coin in my open hand and say to a group of people, "Look, in my hand is a coin," because they see the coin, they do not need faith to accept what I say. But if I put the coin behind my back and say, "In my hand is a coin," they must decide whether or not to accept my word. Because they cannot see it, they must choose to believe or to disbelieve. Their decision will be based on their trust in my word. Their not being able to see the coin does not prove it is not there. It is there, but to know this, they must believe my word.

In the vast unseen world, provisions for every need have been made available through Jesus Christ. The Word of God tells us this. We must choose to believe or to disbelieve God's Word.

Because we do not see these provisions, does not mean they do not exist. They are real, and they are to be laid hold of. Our faith is the evidence of their existence — of their reality. Faith is the evidence of things not seen. God's Word is truth. God does not lie.

He cannot lie (Titus 1:2). His Word is to be trusted. Faith comes through His Word.

2 Kings 6 tells the story of the king of Syria sending a large army with horses and chariots to capture Elisha, the prophet. The army came by night and surrounded the city. Early in the morning, Elisha's servant arose and was alarmed by what he saw. Elisha, however, was not perturbed because he not only saw the natural plane, but he had insight into the spiritual dimension. He said to his servant, *"Do not fear, for those who are with us are more than those who are with them."* Then Elisha prayed and said, *"O Lord, I pray, open his eyes that he may see"* ....(verses 16,17). A strange prayer? No. Elisha was praying that his servant might have spiritual sight. There was another world unseen to him. A real world. Just because the servant could not see it, did not mean it was not there. It was there, but until his spiritual eyes were opened, he could not see. *"And the Lord opened the servant's eyes, and he saw; and behold, the mountain was full of horses and chariots of fire all around Elisha"* (verse 17).

Elisha was a man of faith. His faith related to the unseen world. His faith pleased God and brought angelic deliverance.

Faith the Channel for Receiving

"Now faith is the assurance of things hoped for" ....
Hebrews 11:1

Faith is the channel through which we receive what we are hoping for. Hope and faith work together; but it is through faith that we receive the promises of God

— not through hope. Many Christians think they have faith, when they only have hope.

Hope relates to the future. Faith relates to the present. Hope says, "I will be delivered." Faith says, "I am delivered."

This is not undermining hope. Hope can be defined as a confident, mental expectation of good, and it is extremely important. You will never have faith if you do not have hope (although you can have hope without having faith). I remember once being so despairing that I almost lost every vestige of hope I had. It is terrible to be in a place where you are without hope.

Hope is important, but hope alone is not enough. For years I lived in the future, countless times saying to Shirley, "One day I'm going to be different. One day Jesus will heal me. One day I'm going to be free." But it was always ahead somewhere out of reach, like the proverbial carrot dangled before the donkey. What I thought was faith was only hope.

As you have been reading this book, hope has come to many of you. Your mind has received positive expectations of good and blessing. You are saying, "At last I can see there is an answer for me." If you are now to bring what you are hoping for into your experience, you must channel your hopes through the channel of faith.

"Now may the God of hope fill you with all joy and peace in believing, that you may abound in hope by the power of the Holy Spirit" (Romans 15:13). Some say, "Lord, when I have joy and peace, I will believe," But the Word says to believe and then joy and peace will come. Don't put the cart before the horse.

The Operation of Faith

To operate faith to receive the blessings of God, there are principles we need to know and follow. Of course, through obedience to God, blessings come upon us without our even asking; but the answers to certain physical, mental, and spiritual needs will only be found by pressing into God and receiving them by faith.

Expressed simply, the principles of operating faith are (a) receive by praying, and (b) establish by saying.

In Mark 11, by cursing a barren fig tree, Jesus taught His disciples how to operate faith. Let us look carefully at this passage:

And on the next day, when they had departed from Bethany, He became hungry.

And seeing at a distance a fig tree in leaf, He went to see if perhaps He would find anything on it; and when He came to it, He found nothing but leaves, for it was not the season for figs.

And He answered and said to it, "May no one ever eat fruit from you again!" And His disciples were listening.

● ● ● ● ● ● ●

And whenever evening came, they would go out of the city.

And as they were passing by in the morning, they saw the fig tree withered from the roots up.

And being reminded, Peter said to Him, "Rabbi, behold, the fig tree which You cursed has withered."

And Jesus answered saying to them, "Have faith in God.

Truly I say to you, whoever says to this mountain,

*'Be taken up and cast into the sea,' and does not doubt
in his heart, but believes that what he says is going
to happen, it shall be granted him.*

*Therefore I say to you, all things for which you pray
and ask, believe that you have received them, and
they shall be granted you."*

Mark 11:12—14; 19—24

(a) Receive by Praying

In the Mark 11 passage just quoted, Jesus said, ... *"all
things for which you pray and ask, believe that you have
received them, and they shall be granted you."* The pro-
gression is (1) "pray and ask," (2) "believe," and (3)
"shall be granted."

(1)   "Pray and ask": Knowing that it is God's will
for us to be free, and knowing that Jesus Christ has provided a complete redemption for us through Calvary,
we are to ask the Father in Jesus' Name for our
deliverance once and for all.

(2)   "Believe": Having asked for the provision,
Jesus said, "Believe you have received." Faith is now.
I believe I have received. Even though I cannot see the
provision, even though I feel unchanged, I believe I
have received. The evidence that the provision is mine
is my faith — faith that has come through the Word.

(3)   "Shall be granted": Shall speaks of the future.
We have already received the provisions by faith; but
they shall be granted at a later time. They are ours now
in the unseen realm, but not yet ours in the seen realm.

Because you have the answer by faith, you no longer
keep asking for it. To keep asking is evidence that you

have not by faith received it. No more asking, but thanking and praising God that what you asked Him for is yours. Faith is your evidence. Faith relates to the unseen realm and "sees" the provision as yours — now!

The Holy Spirit will then release into your experience what you received when you prayed. But time is often involved: perhaps hours, days, months, and sometimes years. In the waiting, testing period, you are to maintain your confession of possession by praise and thanksgiving. If you are merely parroting principles, you will be disappointed; but if you have this truth operating from your spirit, you will receive it in experience no matter how long may be the delay.

Praying with Understanding

Understanding this faith principle was the turning point for me. Thousands upon thousands of times I had asked the Lord for healing and deliverance, but never had I believed that I had received the answer. Now I came to the Lord to make one final request. When I began to pray, my imagination came alive. In the heavenlies I saw an enormous "bank" with every provision (blessing gained through the Cross) for the human race, and I saw a small account with my name on it. As I asked, believing I was receiving, I envisaged the Lord taking from His vast bank a small amount of provision — the answer to my small needs — and placing it in my personal account. The answer was mine! Healing, deliverance — mine! Not yet in earthly experience, but in heavenly places. Why? Because I believed I had received it when I prayed. What was my evidence? Faith in my heart. It was faith that was to increase as I continued to meditate upon the Mark 11 passage, and daily thank the Lord (no more asking) for what I had received by faith.

My prayer went something like this: "Heavenly Father, I have asked so many times that You would change me, deliver me. But now I see that I have not been releasing faith. I have been putting the responsibility on You to change me, while all the time You have been waiting for me to use my faith to partake of what Jesus gained for me at Calvary. Lord, I come to ask You one final time. Please set me free from the bondages of the enemy. I ask You in Jesus' Name for this provision. Lord, I receive my deliverance now. I receive complete salvation for every part of me. Your Word says: 'When you pray and ask, believe you have received,' and I believe, and I now receive. The provision is now in my account in the heavenlies. I never need ask again. I praise You. I thank You. By faith I am totally free. The bands of darkness are loosed. I am free! Jesus, my Deliverer! Thank You.''

When I prayed this with understanding, something happened inside me. The victory that was always ahead of me came into my spirit. Deep inside I knew the victory was mine, even though I was still just as bound. Now I was going to battle Satan's demons, not for the victory, but from the victory. Never again did I ask God for my deliverance. I simply kept thanking Him that it was mine.

When this turning point came, I was feeling very low, and apart from an awareness of victory in my spirit, I remained feeling low. I continued thanking God for the victory for three weeks before I noticed any change. When it came, it was very, very small, and yet it was a change — just a minute awareness that I was a little freer. I was encouraged to keep moving on in faith. I had received by praying, and Jesus had said that if I did that, then the provision would be granted.

"That you may not be sluggish, but imitators of those who through faith and patience inherit the promises" (Hebrews 6:12).

(b) Establish by Saying

Weeks and months went by. Slowly I became stronger in myself, yet not much freer. It was then that the Lord taught me that by intelligently engaging in spiritual warfare, I could work with Him to release His answer more quickly. Certainly, by faith, I had received Calvary's provisions; yet I was still very bound.

Five years previously, spirits had come to the surface in an evident way with cryings and tearings in my body, but excepting for a few occasions, they had since "lain low." They had hidden themselves, and at times had even tried to tell me, via thoughts in my mind that they were not there.

Now my confession expanded. Instead of just thanking the Lord for freedom, I confronted the hidden strongholds. I named the areas of bondage and declared them defeated. I commanded spirits of darkness to leave me declaring they now had no legal ground in my life. For some months I continued in warfare in this way without outward manifestations, but gradually noticed more freedom coming.

Discernings of spirits

Then came a further turning point in which the Lord gave me clearer insight into how to break demonic strongholds. As I maintained my confession of faith and declaration that the works of Satan had no part in me, I began to "see" what was happening inside me. I became aware of the names of the spirits that God was dealing with as I prayed. I "saw" their reactions, their resistings, their weakenings' and their breaking up. As spirits rose and left me, I "saw" them going. Before long I realised that the gift of "discernings of spirits" was beginning to operate in my life.

Through this the Lord has taught me from personal experience how to successfully overcome satanic bondages. One important thing I learned was the power of speaking to areas of bondage and in Jesus' Name commanding release. I saw how the spirits reacted to the words I spoke.

There is tremendous power in the spoken word. God created the world simply by speaking words. He rules the entire universe by the power of His word. If He chose to, He could speak one word and the entire universe would be obliterated. Jesus spoke to the wind and the storm and it instantly obeyed Him. He healed and delivered by speaking words. We launch our spiritual weapons through speaking.

In the Scripture passage under consideration, the fig tree withered and died because Jesus spoke to it. Our faith is to be released in words and actions. Jesus said, ... *"May no one ever eat fruit from you again!"* And His disciples were listening. Why? Because Jesus was speaking.

The next day when they again passed the fig tree, Peter expressed amazement that it had withered and died. Jesus replied with these powerful words: ...."*Have faith in God. Truly I say to you, whoever says to this mountain, 'Be taken up and cast into the sea,' and does not doubt in his heart, but believes that what he says is going to happen* (literally, 'believes that what he says happens') *it shall be granted him*" (Mark 11:22,23).

Probably, as He spoke, Jesus turned to a nearby mountain; not that He meant us to remove literal mountains, but He was highlighting the fact that anything — any kind of obstacle — could be removed by the word of faith. Even though the sickness or bondage may seem as immovable as a solid mountain, yet when the "mountain" is spoken to in Jesus' Name, with the speaker not doubting, but believing that what he says is happening as he says it, it shall be removed — what the person says shall indeed happen!

What is said now is one of the most important things in the book:

As you confront demonic bondages, speaking in Jesus' Name, and using the weapons of your warfare, you must believe that what you say, happens. It is happening as you say it. Faith is NOW!

The Measure of Faith

Remember the measure of faith. Our measures are different. Yours may be greater than mine, but we can each use what we have. Because Jesus had the Holy

Spirit without measure (John 3:34), He also had the gift of faith without measure. He could move a mountain with one word. You and I may not be able to move mountains as quickly as Jesus did, but we can get the same results by removing them little by little using the measure of faith we have. As you speak the word of faith to the demonic strongholds, you could perhaps see yourself moving the mountain with a bulldozer, or if your measure of faith is not great enough for that, then see yourself moving it with a pick and shovel. The key is: believe that what you say happens. This is releasing your faith. This is how you please God. Strongholds are weakened and broken by this means. You do not have to feel full of power or tremendously spiritual. Feelings do not come into it. It is by faith we overcome.

If you intelligently confront the source of your problem (your mountain), using your weapons of warfare, and believing that the Holy Spirit is taking your commands and quickening them to be powerful, and believing that what you say is happening as you say it, and continuing day by day to confront and move the mountain, then little by little it will fall away. Slowly and surely your faith will flatten the great mountain.

God said to His people:

Behold, I have made you a new, sharp threshing sledge with double edges;
You will thresh the mountains, and pulverize them,
And will make the hills like chaff.
You will winnow them, and the wind will carry them away,
And the storm will scatter them;
But you will rejoice in the Lord,

You will glory in the Holy One of Israel.

Isaiah 41:15,16

What is the way to remove mountains of fear? Pray and receive your deliverance, by faith, and then speak to the fears in Jesus' Name. Determine from this day on to be a doormat to fear no longer, but to rise up and tread upon the enemy, boldly speaking to the mountains and experiencing them disintegrate before your faith-filled words.

Start speaking to the mountain!

Chapter 9

Launching Spiritual Weapons

Removing mountains of fear and other afflictions is accomplished by the launching of spiritual weapons. As already stated, these **weapons are launched through our mouths,** and are "divinely powerful" for the destruction of demonic fortresses or "mountains".

For though we walk in the flesh, we do not war according to the flesh,

for the weapons of our warfare are not of the flesh, but divinely powerful for the destruction of fortresses. We are destroying speculations and every lofty thing raised up against the knowledge of God, and we are taking every thought captive to the obedience of Christ.

2 Corinthians 10:3—5

Just knowing about these weapons does not bring freedom, but the launching of them does. As they are used, by faith, we will quickly discover just how powerful they are. Let us consider some of them.

The Name of Jesus Christ

Jesus Christ holds the position of supreme authority and power in the visible and invisible realms. 1 Peter 3:22, speaking of Jesus, says, *"who is at the right hand of God, having gone into heaven, after angels and authorities and powers had been subjected to Him."* Colossians 1:15—17 further states that .... *"He is the image of the invisible God, the first-born of all creation. For in Him all things were created, both in the heavens and on earth, visible and invisible, whether thrones or dominions or rulers or authorities — all things have been created through Him and for Him. And He is before all things, and in Him all things hold together"*

Because the Father has bestowed upon His Son "the name which is above every name" (Philippians 2:9), and because Jesus has commissioned us to go in His Name representing Him in the earth (Mark 16:15—20), we have, as Christians, the great privilege of speaking words of life in the Name of Jesus Christ.

Two months ago I joined a fellow minister and his wife to pray for a man who had been ill with cancer for some time. We laid hands upon him, and, in the Name of Jesus Christ, cursed the disease and commanded spirits of infirmity and death to leave his body. As we did so, the Holy Spirit took our words and quickened them to be divinely powerful to the destruction of the affliction. The power of God went through his body and he was aware of a supernatural impartation. Upon returning to his doctor and after undergoing tests, no trace of cancer could be found anywhere. He had been healed, by words of faith spoken in the Name of Jesus Christ.

As we confront strongholds of the enemy, we are to confront them, not in our name, or in the name of our church, but in the Name of Jesus Christ, the Son of God.

The Word of God

The Word of God is also called the Sword of the Spirit (Ephesians 6:17). A sword is a thrusting, striking, blade which, when skilfully handled, becomes a deadly weapon. The Word of God is such a weapon in spiritual realms. As we speak God's Word, we are confronting enemy strongholds, and in effect, parrying, piercing and prevailing over spiritual powers. In the incident just mentioned, we laid our hands on the man for thirty minutes or so, and, using God's Word as a sword, we cursed the cancer in Jesus' Name. It was only as spirits left that healing virtue could flow, and, in his case, it came like charges of power flowing through his whole body. Often we are praying for healing when we should first be driving out the spirits. Deal with the spirits and then the healing can flow.

Whether we quote Bible verses or paraphrase the truths of God's Word as we wield the Sword of the Spirit, we can only do so because we are familiar with the Scriptures. Jesus Himself, when tempted by Satan, overcame every attack with the declaration of God's Word (Luke 4:1—13).

When ministering to believers, I like to come against spirits of fear with words something like this: "We destroy your works now. You have no legal ground to afflict this person any longer." By speaking of "no legal ground" we are declaring that we know our rights as declared in the Word of God. We know what Jesus has accomplished through His death and resurrection. We know it is God's will for us to be free. We know that evil spirits are squatters and are defeated foes having no right to occupy areas of our lives. We know what the Word says and speak it out boldly.

The Blood of Christ

Undoubtedly the most powerful substance that has ever touched the soil of this planet is the blood of Jesus Christ. Through centuries, the blood of countless animals had been shed to fulfil the demands of the Law of God for His people to be made righteous. But in Christ as the Lamb of God, all old Testament types and pictures found their fulfilment. When He offered Himself up to be put to death after having lived a sinless life, He became a perfect sacrifice, totally acceptable to His Father. The shedding of His blood not only brought to an end the need for animal sacrifices, but also provided a way for all men to be forgiven their sins, and to be restored to a right relationship with God (Hebrews 9,10). By His death He fully satisfied the legal requirements of the Law.

As a result, Satan's "legal" stronghold and domination over man has been broken. Whenever a man hears the good news of Christ's death, repents of his sinful ways, and yields himself to the Lordship of Christ, the shed blood of Jesus avails for him, providing an instant release from the legal requirements of the Law (Romans 5:6—21). To announce what the blood of Jesus has accomplished is to launch the most powerful weapon against the strongholds of the enemy.

Revelation 12:11 speaks of believers overcoming

Satan in this way. *"And they overcame him (Satan) because of the blood of the Lamb and because of the word of their testimony"* ....

We too overcome Satan and break free from the shackles of fear and other afflictions by testifying to what the Word of God says the Blood of Jesus Christ has accomplished.

(1) I am brought near to God by the blood of Jesus.
(Ephesians 2:13)

(2) I am cleansed from all sin by the blood of Jesus.
(1 John 1:7)

(3) I am justified by the blood of Jesus.
(Romans 5:8,9)

(4) I have redemption through the blood of Jesus.
(Ephesians 1:7)

(5) I am healed by the blood of Jesus.(1 Peter 2:24)

(6) I have peace with God through the blood of Jesus. (Colossians 1:20)

(7) I am purchased by the blood of Jesus.
(Acts 20:28)

(8) I have confidence to come into the presence of God by the blood of Jesus.
(Hebrews 10:19—22)

(9) I am in covenant relationship with God through the blood of Jesus. (Mark 14:24)

(10) I am sanctified through the blood of Jesus.
(Hebrews 13:12)

(11) The blood of Jesus cleanses my conscience.
(Hebrews 9:14)

(12) The blood of Jesus is precious to me.
(1 Peter 1:19)

The Spirit of God

As we speak in Jesus' Name, as we declare what the Word says, as we testify to what the blood of Jesus Christ has accomplished, the Spirit of God quickens what we say and makes our words powerful and life-giving. 2 Corinthians 3:6 says, ... *"the letter kills but the Spirit gives life."*

It was only after Jesus had been filled with the Holy Spirit that He commenced His public ministry, preaching, delivering, and healing (Matthew 3:16).

The Lord Jesus was totally dependent upon the Holy Spirit as the source of His power to do the works of God. Although the Son of God, He chose to lay aside His glory and power while He walked this earth, and depend utterly upon the Spirit of God (Philippians 2:5—8). Acts 10:36 says: *"You know of Jesus of Nazareth, how God anointed Him with the Holy Spirit and with power, and how He went about doing good, and healing all who were oppressed by the devil; for God was with Him."*

When Jesus was criticised by the Pharisees for casting out demons by the power of Beelzebub He responded by saying, ..."*if Satan casts out Satan, he is divided against himself; how then shall his kingdom stand?"* He then continued, *"but if I cast out demons by the Spirit of God, then the kingdom of God has come upon you"* (Matthew 12:26,28). The Luke account of this accusation and response says, *"but if I cast out demons by the finger of God, then the kingdom of God has come upon you"* (Luke 11:20).

As we come against spirits of fear in Jesus' Name,

let us realise it is the gracious ministry of the Spirit of God who energises our words and brings to fulfilment what we say.

Praise

Earlier this year I walked into an auditorium where a camp had just concluded. The pastor expressed joyfully that one of the meetings during the camp had been given to praising and worshipping the Lord. There had been no preaching, just exalting Jesus, and this had gone on for some hours. What had happened? The anointing of God settled upon the people and wonderful deliverances and healings had occurred. No pleading for God to work. Just praising Him for His Presence and that He was working. There is power in praise.

As we speak or sing praise to God, we are launching yet further missiles against enemy strongholds. Today is a day of restoration in the Church, and part of the restoring of that which had been lost is an emphasis on praise and worship. Churches that are released in this dimension are churches where God is meeting the needs of people, for as He is exalted, a way is made for Him to manifest His Presence.

It was midnight, and Paul and Silas were in an inner prison with their feet fastened in stocks. This had been their reward for setting a girl free from a spirit of divination. However, as they chose to praise God and not to feel sorry for themselves, they were marvellously delivered.

"But about midnight Paul and Silas were praying and singing hymns of praise to God, and the prisoners were

listening to them; and suddenly there came a great earthquake, so that the foundations of the prison house were shaken; and immediately all the doors were opened, and everyone's chains were unfastened" (Acts 16:25,26).

As we learn to truly praise God we will discover the power of His Spirit breaking the demonic chains, undoing demonic stocks and setting us free even in the darkest hour.

Praise brings deliverance. David the Psalmist sang ....*"Thou art holy, O thou who art enthroned upon the praises of Israel"* (Psalm 22:3). Indeed God enthrones Himself, God dwells, God inhabits, the praises of His people.

Speaking in Tongues

On the day of Pentecost the gathered disciples were filled with the Holy Spirit and began speaking with other tongues as the Spirit gave them utterance (Acts 2:3,4). This amazed the multitude who heard them in their own languages ....*"speaking of the mighty deeds of God"* (Acts 2:11).

God is pouring out His Spirit all over the world today and millions of Christians know what it is to be released to praise God in languages they have never learned. What a wonderful blessing it is to exalt God in this way and to experience a new dimension of spiritual reality and communion with Him (1 Corinthians 14:2,14,15).

When a person speaks in tongues he is edifying or building himself up. *"One who speaks in a tongue edifies himself"* .... (1 Corinthians 14:4). Part of this edification process is for the Holy Spirit to speak words of release from demonic bondages as was so clearly evidenced when the Lord released me in the Maori language last year while in New Zealand. As I commanded in tongues, evil spirits were confronted in the mother tongue of the people being ministered to, and bondages were being broken. ....*" 'Not by might nor by power but by My Spirit,' says the Lord of hosts"* (Zechariah 4:6).

As you speak to mountains of fear in your life there is a time to command in tongues, a time to praise in tongues, a time to release the Holy Spirit to work in ways that bypass the limitations of your own mind. Great devastation is wrought upon demonic strongholds as you speak in tongues.

Confession of Identification

As we harmonise our hearts and lips with what the Word of God declares we have become in Jesus Christ, our Great High Priest is released in His heavenly ministry before the Father on our behalf (Hebrews 7:23—26; 8:1,2).

"Therefore, holy brethren, partakers of a heavenly calling, consider Jesus, the Apostle and High Priest of our confession" (Hebrews 3:1). The word confession is the Greek "homologeo", which means literally, "to speak the same thing". As the High Priest of our confession He makes our declarations known to the Father. With this action of mediation is released the dynamic of the Holy Spirit's ministry, to make real in our

experience that which we confess.

Our confession can go like this:

In Christ my sinful nature has been crucified.
                                        Romans 6:6
In Christ my sinful nature has been buried.
                                        Romans 6:4
In Christ I have been raised to newness of life.
                                        Romans 6:5
In Christ I have ascended to the right hand of the
Father.   Ephesians 2:6
In Christ I have been made complete.
                                        Colossians 2:10
In Christ I reign in life through the abundance of
God's grace.   Romans 5:17
In Christ FEAR HAS NO PLACE IN ME. Timothy 1:7

As we launch this confession of freedom from fear because we are believers in Jesus Christ, powerful missiles are released to weaken and pulverise every mountain of fear.

Start confessing today what you are in Christ.

Gifts of The Holy Spirit

"Now concerning spiritual gifts, brethren, I do not want you to be unaware" (1 Corinthians 12:1). "Unaware" in the Greek means "not to know (through lack of information), or to ignore (through disinclination)".

In this chapter Paul mentions nine gifts or manifestations of the Holy Spirit. These gifts must operate today if we are to be successful in evangelising our nation and the world. There are:

3 Power Gifts: faith, healings, the effecting of miracles.

112

3 Utterance Gifts: prophecy, tongues, interpretation of tongues.

3 Revelation Gifts: word of wisdom, word of knowledge, discernings of spirits.

The Revelation Gifts are particularly valuable in dealing with unseen demonic powers binding lives. Through "words of knowledge" for example, the Holy Spirit reveals information about a person's life or needs that enables the counsellor to move quickly and ably in dealing with a problem.

Through "discernings of spirits" one is able to "see" or "perceive" the presence of evil spirits; to know their names; to recognise the strength of the bondage area; to follow their reactions and weakenings as they are bound and commanded to go; to perceive them leaving a person; to know what other spirits are closely associated with those being dealt with; and to recognise whether the holds are partially or totally broken.

Recently we were ministering to a group of missionaries and praying for them one by one to be set free. When it came time for one woman to be prayed for, she expressed a desire for prayer but also a lack of awareness of any area of bondage in her life. Her openness to the ministry of the Holy Spirit released the gifts of the Holy Spirit to flow.

Immediately I discerned spirits of the fear of death and began to command them to leave her life. To her surprise and joy she began to be delivered from longstanding fears that had gripped her life from childhood. By discernings of spirits numerous fears were identified, and by words of knowledge how they entered was established. At one point I declared that

Jesus was delivering her from the fear of being raped. After the session had concluded, she told us that two weeks earlier she had asked for prayer for this very area of need.

This fine Christian leader, who had been raised in a nation that has experienced much violence and bloodshed, and had been exposed to many fears and bondages, simply because of the environment in which she grew up.

By asking the Holy Spirit for supernatural revelation and by speaking that revelation — by launching it through our mouths — demonic bondages are destroyed in Jesus' Name. Hallelujah!

Chapter 10

How Spirits Leave

As believers take their God-given authority and renounce the workings of spirits of fear in their lives, as they launch spiritual missiles through their mouths, as faith is involved in their actions, the Holy Spirit is released to work and drive out the spirits.

Marksmen are skilful at focusing on their targets and then releasing their bullets with lethal accuracy. As we confront spirits of fear we need to "sight in" upon them. If you are struggling with the fear of rejection, you don't need some special revelation to know with what you have to deal. You already know. It may be helpful to actually write down the areas of fear you need to overcome, realising there are spirits behind each area.

Direct Confrontation

When Jesus confronted evil spirits He was very forthright.

And Jesus rebuked him, saying, "Be quiet and come out of him!" ....

Luke 4:35

...."Come out of the man, you unclean spirit!"

Mark 5:8

....He rebuked the unclean spirit, saying to it, "You deaf and dumb spirit, I command you, come out of him and do not enter him again" .

Mark 9:25

Paul was similarly bold ....*Paul was greatly annoyed, and turned and said to the spirit, "I command you in the name of Jesus Christ to come out of her!"* ....

Acts 16:18

We are commanded to "cast out demons" in Jesus' Name (Mark 16:17). The words "cast out" are translated from the Greek word "ekballo", which is a very aggressive word meaning "to eject, cast forth, cast out, drive out, expel, pluck out, pull out, take out, thrust out, put out, send away, send out". Obviously there is no place for passivity when confronting demons.

Types of Manifestations

Often as evil spirits leave, their goings are accompanied by manifestations, sometimes mild, sometimes traumatic.

And while the sun was setting, all who had any sick with various diseases brought them to Him; and .laying His hands on every one of them, He was healing them.

And demons also were coming out of many, crying out and saying, "You are the Son of God!" And rebuking them, He would not allow them to speak, because they knew Him to be the Christ.

Luke 4:40,41

And just then there was in their synagogue a man with an unclean spirit; and he cried out,

116

saying, "What do we have to do with You, Jesus of Nazareth? Have You come to destroy us? I know who You are — the Holy One of God!"

And Jesus rebuked him, saying, "Be quiet, and come out of him!"

And throwing him into convulsions, the unclean spirit cried out with a loud voice, and came out of him.

Mark 1:23—26

And when Jesus saw that a crowd was rapidly gathering, He rebuked the unclean spirit, saying to it, "You deaf and dumb spirit, I command you, come out of him and do not enter him again."

And after crying out and throwing him into terrible convulsions, it came out; and the boy became so much like a corpse that most of them said, "He is dead!"

But Jesus took him by the hand and raised him; and he got up.

Mark 9:25—27

And Philip went down to the city of Samaria and began proclaiming Christ to them.

And the multitudes with one accord were giving attention to what was said by Philip, as they heard and saw the signs which he was performing.

For in the case of many who had unclean spirits, they were coming out of them shouting with a loud voice; and many who had been paralyzed and lame were healed.

And there was much rejoicing in that city.

Acts 8:5—8

We should not be afraid of such manifestations but rejoice at the demonstration of God's power at such a time. Spirits are afraid of being exposed and afraid of being evicted from their "homes", and cry out in fear at the power of Jesus Christ released against them.

Traumatic Manifestations may take the following forms:
— an inward or outward physical tearing
— throwing around or to the ground
— foaming at the mouth, vomiting
— resisting, violent action, supernatural strength
— crying out, cursing, vile utterances

Mild Manifestations might include:
— sighing, coughing, belching, yawning
— breathing heavily, tightness or pressure points
— inward stirrings
— feeling spirits rising and leaving with the breath

Imperceptible Manifestations
— no awareness, physically or emotionally of spirits leaving
— perhaps a spiritual perception of a releasing

During a time of deliverance, it is possible to experience manifestations in any of the above categories but often deliverance is not accompanied by aggressive manifestations. It is important to realise they can occur and to be prepared and not fearful. On the other hand no visible manifestations does not mean deliverance has not taken place. Many major and life changing releases have taken place without "feelings" being experienced, or outward signs being evidenced.

Evicted Through the Mouth

The word "spirit" in both the Hebrew and Greek languages can also be translated "wind" or "breath."

Spirits then can be likened to wind or breath. We read of the angels of God, who are spirit beings, in Hebrews 1:7. ...."*who makes His angels winds, and His ministers a flame of fire.*"

Many spirits enter through the mouth and also leave through the mouth. In the Scriptures just quoted we read expressions such as:

And demons also were **coming out of many, crying out** .... Luke 4:41

And throwing him into convulsions, the unclean spirit **cried out with a loud voice, and came out of him.** Mark 1:26

And **after crying out** *and throwing him into terrible convulsions,* **it came out** .... Mark 9:26

For in the case of many who had unclean spirits, **they were coming out of them shouting with a loud voice** .... Acts 8:7

When spirits cry out, they do so using the vocal chords and mouth of the person afflicted. They rise with the breath and are expelled through the mouth. Not all spirits enter and leave this way, but most do, as is evidenced by the many whose deliverance is character-ised by some outward manifestation. This is why when commanding spirits to leave I say, "Come out now, in Jesus' Name, coming up and out with the natural breath."

Perseverance Required

A weak hold can be broken easily but a strong hold usually takes much time to destroy. Spirits know there is strength in numbers and therefore gather in groupings. This is why perseverance in warfare over extended periods of time is essential to effect complete and permanent deliverance.

It is only as some strongholds are confronted on a consistent basis, that one realises just how strong the holds are. Many persons are riddled with inferiority and insecurity, for instance, traits inspired by spirits that have become so much a part of the personality, that it is hard to know what the person is really like. As spiritual weapons are released in faith however, the person will notice a wonderful transformation taking place within, and will be delighted at the "new creation" he is becoming in Christ.

Mark 5 tells of Jesus setting a deranged man free. Although He confronted the spirits initially in the singular, when the spokesman of the group indicated there were thousands of them (a Roman legion consisted of between three thousand and six thousand men), He spoke to them in the plural. When commanding spirits to go, if I speak to them in the singular I am always thinking in the plural because I know so well how they operate. Also, through discernings of spirits, one is only too aware that we are dealing with numbers of spirits of the same kind and not just a single intruder. Speak in the singular (or plural) but think in the plural.

Releasing Your Faith

As you confront 'mountains' of fear in your own life, using your powerful spiritual weaponry, let your natural breathing out be the point of contact for releasing your faith. You can say to the demons: "In Jesus' Name I break your hold. Come up and out of your hiding places now. I drive you out. As I breathe, you are going. I expel you with the breath." Simply believe that what you say is happening.

Sometimes when spirits are leaving, the person breathes deeply and heavily. This excessive expulsion of breath is not done by the person, but is caused by the spirits as they are stirred up and leave. When this happens regularly, a person may feel that to hasten the deliverance, heavy breathing is helpful the whole of the prayer time. This is not advisable, however, because continued heavy breathing can cause dizziness.

On the other hand, when spirits are stirring and coming out, it sometimes helps to have a period of "pushing out," when you purposely push from your stomach region and breath out heavily pushing your breath up and out. Times of expulsion like this, when you aggressively stir yourself to expel demons, can be helpful. Generally, however, breathing should be natural and relaxed.

Commanding Inwardly

When you are commanding, it is not always necessary to speak to demons audibly. Inward commanding (speaking in your mind without speaking through your lips) is just as effective. In fact, often it is more effective.

Sometimes, as you declare audibly the power of the Blood, or as you praise God, the spirits will rise, but not get past your lips. Your praise or your declaration actually becomes a barrier to their expulsion. In such situations, quiet, inward commands are entirely appropriate

In a counselling situation, I encourage the counsellee to concentrate on inward commands, using spiritual weapons inwardly while I and any other counsellor make audible outward commands. From personal experience, and by perceiving through the discernings of spirits, I have learned that under normal circumstances more results are achieved this way than by having the counsellee totally involved in outward renunciation.

Although I have the counsellee major on the inward, I usually commence a deliverance session by asking him to audibly renounce the works of the enemy and confess Jesus Christ to be his Lord. Every so often during the session, I encourage the person to join in with specific, audible commands and declarations. In this way he learns self-deliverance, a necessary activity in maintaining personal deliverance, as well as later, ministry to others.

Sometimes while people are commanding inwardly, I perceive that the spirits will only come out after the person has made a bold, audible renunciation of them. At times like this the person's involvement is essential.

This mixture of inward and outward commands, in conjunction with breathing out as a point of contact for releasing your faith, is one of the most important things this book will impart in helping you deliver yourself.

For those of you who will be being set free without traumatic or mild manifestations, we thought it would be encouraging for you to read the testimony of a very dear friend and colleague of ours in Australia, Daphne Drummond. Her testimony is taken from the last chapter of CHRISTIAN SET YOURSELF FREE, where a number of people tell their stories. Notice, particularly, the persistence involved as she dealt with the bondage area. Daphne's story deals with freedom from fear, but let her speak for herself.

A Lifetime of Nightmares Broken
Daphne Drummond

To give you some idea of the power that fear had in my life, I will have to take you back to my early childhood. I was born in India where my father was an electrical and consulting engineer. At the time of my birth he had designed and was supervising the construction of an electrical plant for His Highness, the Maharajah of Bikaner. This meant that my parents lived a very social life, and we children were frequently left in the care of the Indian servants.

We were strictly brought up and one of the rules was: to bed at six o'clock winter and summer. At six o'clock in summer, with the sun still up, it was hard for children to go to bed. To make us go, the Indian servants would threaten us: "If you don't get into bed, the jackals or the tigers will get you!" When this did not work, they would hide on the stairway and make animal noises. By this time it was normally dark, and I would spring into bed, put the sheet over my head and lie still, almost too frightened to breathe. Any minute I expected the tiger to spring onto my bed and devour me. I was petrified. This happened night after night, and my little heart would almost jump out of my body with fear.

If it was not the servants frightening us, it was snakes. We children were not allowed out of bed until our slippers had been searched for snakes and scorpions. Thus at an early age, fear took hold of my life, and as far back as I can remember, I suffered from nightmares.

One day, as punishment for being disobedient, my parents went out with my sister and left me home with the Indian servants. Our bearer went out and came back with an Indian who was brandishing a huge scythe and threatening to kill me. The bearer pretended to struggle with him and eventually got him to go. I froze on the spot; I was terrified; my eyes must have been as large as saucers, and my heart was pounding. The bearer came back with his finger bandaged up saying, "Look what he did to me as I struggled to save you!" I stood, unable to move. Our parents did not know what was going on. We never reported the servants. This we were never encouraged to do.

India to Australia

The fears began to plague me, increasing as I grew older. When I came to Australia at nine years of age, I would not go into a dark room and switch on the light, much to the disgust of my mother's relatives with whom we were staying. They called me a coward. A girl my age too frightened to put on a light!

As I grew up, the nightmares increased. I accepted

them as something I could not do anything about. At the age of eighteen, when I became a Christian, I began to pray about the nightmares, never going to bed without asking the Lord to keep me from them, even pleading the Blood upon myself.

China Call

As time went on, I felt the call of God to go to China as a missionary. In preparation, I went to Bible School and there the nightmares intensified and became more frightening. Every night I would dream of demons. Some nights they would be sitting on my chest, trying to press the breath out of my body, and saying they were going to kill me. In my sleep I would be paralyzed. Struggling to wake up, there would be a voice within me saying, "The Blood! The Blood!" When I eventually woke up, I would be in a bath of perspiration, my heart pounding, and a physical pain of tension gripping my stomach. These constant dreams left me exhausted. There were times when I sat up late, almost too frightened to go to bed.

Having prayed about it, but still feeling distressed, I talked to one of our pastors who had been used in the deliverance ministry in Scotland during a revival there. He said to me, "Daphne, I guarantee that if you gave up your call to China, got yourself a job, and settled back to ordinary life again, those dreams would cease." Be that as it may, I was setting my goals towards China, and not even these dreams would deter me.

I went to China with the fears still troubling me in my dreams. Many of them were so vivid, I would have to get up, turn on the light, walk about, and wake myself up. Otherwise I would go back to sleep and continue on where the dreams left off. They were draining my strength. Of course, China was no country to cure fears. Before I went, a retired missionary had told me to be prepared to lose everything at least once during my missionary life. They had been robbed of everything three times.

We were "bandit conscious." When leaving us on our own, our superintendent always said, "If the bandits come, don't try to intercept them. Let them take what they like. Your life is worth more than money or goods." We used to go to bed with a kerosene lamp and our Chinese dress by our bed in case we had to get up in a hurry. One person was always responsible to be on guard. One of our missionaries was stabbed when trying to intercept bandits.

Leaving China

When I came out of China, having to flee because of the Communist takeover, the pattern of my nightmares changed. Now is was Chinese bandits chasing me. They would be around every corner coming towards me with knives, or down a dark tunnel. It was either bandits or snakes. The snakes were so numerous that I could not tread anywhere without stepping on them. Some were huge, their jaws open within inches of my face, ready to swallow me. I would wake up in a bath of perspiration with my heart racing, and the fear pain in my stomach. It troubled me and I wondered what I could do. I had prayed about it and used the Blood so often, yet nothing seemed to work. I tried to overcome it with all the will power I had, but to no avail.

In 1977, after many years home in Australia, I moved to another city not knowing what God had for me, and was quite surprised when the door opened and I was plunged into the ministry of deliverance. Pastor Graham Powell approached me and invited me to join him when praying for women. He had been praying for someone to join him, and my name had come to his mind. This is how God began to teach me, and I here wish to thank God for Pastor Powell's ministry and all He taught me through him.

Deliverance at Last

One day I happened to mention that I was plagued with nightmares; so Graham offered to pray with me. He began to pray against spirits of fear. As he prayed I felt absolutely nothing. There were no manifestations, but Graham said he saw spirits leaving me. Three times he prayed for me, and after that I was on my own. When I was travelling on the bus, I would often use the minutes to command the demons of fear to leave. Just quietly under my breath I would command them to leave in the Name of Jesus. It was an exercise of faith, because I did not feel anything stirring inside, nor did I have any outward indication that they were leaving.

At first I did not understand why it was necessary to keep on daily commanding. Previously, the only understanding I had of deliverance was what I had seen a few times at altar calls, and read about. The idea had formed in my mind that they came out at the first command, and you were then free.

However, I had an open mind to the new things I was learning — and there was much to learn. In faith I continued commanding them to leave. After a while I began to notice that the nightmares were becoming wider apart. I might go for two weeks and not have any.

The question is often asked: "How do you know when you are delivered?" How do you know when you are well when you go to a doctor? By losing your pains and aches and symptoms. I watched the "symptoms" become less frequent and less violent in nature, and it was by this that I knew God was delivering me. It is good to stop now and again, and look back and see how far the Lord has brought you. You see a big change.

Still I kept on, and it did not take long to learn that there is not only one demon to drive out, but many. At first I could not understand this, but now I know by experience. They do not come in by ones, but by many. They set up quite a colony — even in one area — and it is "demons" you are dealing with, not just "a demon."

I constantly commanded in faith, not feeling anything; but it was evident that something wonderful was happening. I was waking in the morning not feeling worn out. It was marvellous to get a good night's sleep after years of waking up feeling I had not gone to bed. At the end of about three months, the nightmares ceased, and what a joy filled my heart to know that deliverance is for today and is real. I might add that towards the end I began to yawn a few times. This was the first outward sign I had had that the demons were leaving me.

Our total redemption for the spirit, soul, and body was won on Calvary. If we receive salvation by faith, then deliverance is by faith too. It is part of Jesus' great commission in Mark 16:15—18. First to preach the gospel (salvation), second to baptise (water baptism), and third to cast out demons (deliverance). It is God's desire to see His people free, and it can be a reality. God has given us the "keys of the Kingdom." Faith turns the key. I found that God was putting the "key" into my hand, saying, "Deliver yourself," and I had to rise up and use it.

Because I knew so little about deliverance, I began to search the Word with an open mind and many scriptures opened up to me. They became quickened to my heart by the Holy Spirit and these I used in faith. As time went on, my faith began to grow and I was being launched into a deliverance ministry for other people. Demons are real — and so is deliverance. God is still on the throne. Faith brings God into action, and demons flee before His presence. (End quote).

How do we break free from fear? Let us summarise what we have learned.

Firstly: Acknowledge your need of deliverance from fear.

Secondly: Recognise you are bound by spirits of fear.

Thirdly: Yield to Jesus Christ as Lord and Saviour.

Fourthly: Look to Jesus Christ as The Deliverer.

Fifthly: Speak to the fear in the Name of Jesus.

Sixthly: Launch your spiritual weapons by faith.

Seventhly: Persist until the fear is completely gone.

Declaration of Deliverance

The following declaration can be made boldly by all who know a personal relationship with God through Jesus Christ, His Son.

Breaking free from bondages will take much more than speaking forth the following words, but they will serve as a guide to those unaccustomed in releasing the ministry of the Holy Spirit in their lives. Let this declaration be a springboard to a season of spiritual warfare and deliverance from spirits binding your life. Take your spiritual weapons and begin to launch them, by faith, against the bondage areas.

"In the Name of Jesus Christ, and as one confessing Christ as Lord and Saviour, I renounce Satan and all his works.

I bind every spirit of fear afflicting my life, (name the fear or fears ....). In Jesus' Name I render you powerless. You have no legal right to afflict me. I am a child of God. My sins have been forgiven. The Blood of Jesus Christ has cleansed me. Therefore I expel you now by the power of the Spirit of God.

Spirits of fear I drive you out. Come out of your hiding places, leaving my mind, my emotions, my will, my body. As I breathe out normally, I expel you with my breath. You are going now. I cast you out. In Jesus' Name I prevail over you. You are coming up and out now with the breath.

Thank you Lord Jesus. You are releasing me now. Your precious Blood has sanctified me. By the anointing of the Holy Spirit the strongholds of fear are weakening and breaking up. You are releasing me now. I praise you Lord Jesus. You are the great Deliverer. Together we prevail over these fears. Hallelujah! Old things have passed away and all things have become new. I am a new creation in You. Your life is my life. Your peace is my peace. The bands of fear are broken forever. Thank you Lord.''

Chapter 11

Walking Fear Free

Now that we understand something of the nature of the conflict we are in, and how spirits of fear gain entrance into our lives, it is important to learn how to walk in the liberty of God. To walk fear free is God's intention for all. We need to remember that evil spirits will seek to take advantage of every "fear situation" that arises in the process of daily living. Since in this life, we will never be free from the attacks of the enemy, learning how we can be set free is one thing; learning to maintain that freedom is equally important. The following are keys to walking fear free.

1. Experience Deliverance from Spirits of Fear

It is imperative that fear in a life be acknowledged and dealt with. If not, no matter how diligently we endeavour to walk with God, we will be troubled again and again by a concealed enemy at work in the soul. At a recent meeting I was asked to minister to a Christian woman who was devastatingly gripped by fear. As I walked up to her, the Holy Spirit showed me, among other things, that she had been raped. So fearful was she of everyone and everything she was unable to respond to my questions, but a friend confirmed what I had sensed was indeed the case, making her afraid of people and places. Her whole countenance portrayed torment. Unless this woman experienced deliverance from spirits of fear, no amount of Bible reading, Church attendance, and other good necessary Christian disciplines would be of lasting benefit.

On many occasions as a young Christian, I literally shook during the course of a meeting as fears manifested in me. If only I had known the source of those manifestations! Before fears began to break in my life, I had attended thousands of meetings or Church services with no significant evidence of change. If we don't deal with the enemy and cast him out, as we have been commanded to do, we must live with the incapacitating results.

2. Cultivate a Growing Relationship with Jesus Christ

Jesus has many titles to express the beauty and glory of His Person, and Prince of Peace is one of them (Isaiah 9:6). To walk in true peace we must come to the source of true peace and partake of His life. The usage of the words "true peace" is deliberate. There is a counterfeit peace that can come through various avenues such as non-Biblical meditation, drug taking, or false religious commitments and experiences. The price of obtaining such peace, which offers no guarantee of continuance, is very high. When Satan grants what we would consider to be blessing, he takes ground in our lives in some other area. He gives nothing for nothing.

In Chapter Four we outlined how a person can commence the Christian walk by a deliberate commitment to Jesus Christ as Lord and Saviour. With the impartation of Life to the human spirit by the Holy Spirit, a life of knowing God and walking with Him starts. But it is only the beginning.

Just as a babe is born into the physical world through a natural birth, and requires nurturing so that life may be maintained and physical growth experienced, so our encounter with Jesus Christ produces a spiritual birth, with parallel requirements in the spiritual dimension.

Our growth in Christ takes place through our reading and meditating on the Scriptures; through our fellowship with Him in prayer and worship; through being linked to fellow Christians in a vital Church life where we are exposed to the ministries God has set in the Church; through obedience to the commandments of God and harmonising with the principles and laws of God's Kingdom. *"For the kingdom of God is .... righteousness and peace and joy in the Holy Spirit"* (Romans 14:17).

3. Clothe Yourself in the Armour of God

Ephesians 6 makes it plain that we are involved in a spiritual conflict, therefore we are urged to ...."*take up the full armour of God, that you may be able to resist in the evil day, and having done everything, to stand firm"* (verse 13). The pieces of armour are likened to that which would have been worn by a Roman soldier of that period.

| Girded Loins | Breastplate | Shod Feet |
| Shield | Helmet | Sword |

Our armour is not natural but spiritual. Not seen but unseen. Each piece represents Christ to us in different aspects.

having girded your loins with **truth**

having put on the breastplate of **righteousness**

having shod your feet with the preparation of the Gospel of **peace**

taking up the shield of **faith**

take the helmet of **salvation**

the sword of the Spirit, which is the **Word of God**

And let us not forget, *"With all prayer and petition pray at all times in the Spirit"* ....(verse 18).

Only as we wear this armour, day and night, are we able to resist the onslaughts of our satanic enemies. But how do we put on the armour? How do we keep it on? Simply by confessing daily that we are now in Christ, and of our standing before the Father through Him. Furthermore, we must confess our victory over the powers of darkness, and that in Christ we are strong, protected, righteous, filled with peace, and kept by His Word, etc.

The night is almost gone, and the day is at hand. Let us therefore lay aside the deeds of darkness and put on the armor of light.

Let us behave properly as in the day, not in carousing and drunkenness, not in sexual promiscuity and sensuality, not in strife and jealousy.

But put on the Lord Jesus Christ, and make no provision for the flesh in regard to its lusts.

Romans 13:12—14

4. Be Filled with the Holy Spirit

And do not get drunk with wine, for that is dissipation, but be filled with the Spirit.''

Being filled with the Holy Spirit is not an option, but a necessity, if we are to harmonise with God's Word and be victorious over Satan and his works.

When stating the spiritual nature of our warfare and the armour God has given for protection, Paul says, ...*"Be strong in the Lord and in the strength of His might"* (Ephesians 6:10).

How are we strong in the Lord? Certainly by wearing the spiritual armour outlined in Ephesians 6, but also by the strengthening and enabling of the Holy Spirit.

After being baptised in water and in the Holy Spirit, Jesus first experienced a time of attack from Satan in which He prevailed by prayer and fasting, by using the Sword of the Spirit, any by relying on the infilling of the Spirit (Matthew 4:1—11).

The early disciples, after the resurrection of Jesus, were commanded by Him to wait for the promise of the Father before evangelising. Acts 1:4. What was the promise of the Father? *"For John baptized with water, but you shall be baptized with the Holy Spirit not many days from now"* (Acts 1:5).

The disciples were once again filled with the Holy Spirit as they sought God in prayer after the persecution of Peter and John (Acts 4:31).

How can we commence the Spirit-filled life as believers? By coming to Jesus the Baptiser in the Holy

Spirit (Luke 3:16), by asking Him to fill us (Luke 11:5—13), and by receiving the Holy Spirit by faith (Galatians 3:5).

If you have never been filled with the Holy Spirit, you, as one confessing Christ as Lord and Saviour, can enter this dimension of life in God right now by expressing the following prayer from your heart:

"Lord Jesus, I acknowledge You as my Lord and Saviour and the source of my strength and victory. I need Your infilling Lord, and right now I ask You to fill me with the Holy Spirit. As I received You as my Lord and Saviour by faith, I now receive the Holy Spirit's infilling by faith. Lord I receive. I receive a fresh impartation of Your Presence and power right now. Thank You Lord Jesus that You are filling me. I praise and worship You with all of my heart."

As we enter the doorway to the Spirit-filled life, a whole new dimension of spiritual reality begins to unfold. We can begin to experience the gifts or manifestations of the Holy Spirit in and through our lives. In Acts we read of those being filled with the Spirit speaking in tongues and glorifying God in this manner (Acts 2:1—16). On another occasion the disciples spoke with tongues and began to prophecy as the Spirit of God came upon them (Acts 19:6). As you receive the infilling of the Holy Spirit, be open to receive, and speak by faith, a language you have never learned, enabling you to praise the Lord more freely.

A few months after turning my life over to Jesus Christ, I asked Him to fill me with the Holy Spirit. It was a wonderful experience in which the Lord and His

Word became so much more real. However, it was some months later that I actually spoke in tongues. As wonderful as my infilling was, I knew nothing about spiritual gifts. As I then became aware of those precious gifts God wishes to give His children, I simply asked Jesus one day for the gift of tongues. As a fellow Christian prayed with me, I found myself praising God in a language of the Spirit. How I thank God for that day and all the blessings that have come my way over the years through this means of not only praising God, but being edified myself (1 Corinthians 14:1—5).

5. Be on the Alert

Any soldier on active duty is naturally on the alert. While on a visit to Northern Ireland, we shopped in Newry, a town where violence has repeatedly flared up. Here we noticed an armoured vehicle stationed conspicuoulsy in the heart of a plaza with its engine running and its personnel on constant alert, ready to speed to the scene should any violence occur.

As Christians we too are to be on the alert, not in the sense of being afraid of the enemy, for we know he is afraid of us, but in the way 1 Peter 5:8 puts it. *"Be of sober spirit, be on the alert. Your adversary, the devil, prowls about like a roaring lion, seeking someone to devour."* The person who is alert will be able to resist any onslaught of fear in the Name of Jesus; he will be able to *"take up the shield of faith"* and *"to extinguish all the flaming missiles of the evil one"* (Ephesians 6:16).

During my early years as a Christian, I struggled

much with condemnation. Every negative thought that entered my mind I confessed as sin, thinking it came from my "own wicked heart". It seemed I was "confessing my sins" on a constant basis and experienced only partially, the reality of being righteous in Christ.

As I was driving through a crowded street one day, and going through the religious ritual of confession once again, I suddenly had a revelation. God alerted me to the fact that the constant barrage of thoughts came, not from myself, but from the enemy. I had been deceived, condemning myself when I should have been resisting the enemy.

Alerted as to the source of the thoughts, I began to resist them, and, over a period of time, broke a major stronghold in my mind that had kept it filled with thoughts not my own for years. Today I enjoy a mind that is free from condemnation. Even so, I am on the alert to deal with every attack that would come against me. Our minds are a major focal point for enemy attack and infiltration.

6. Praise God Continually

"I will bless the Lord at all times; His praise shall continually be in my mouth" (Psalm 34:1). David goes on to say, *"I sought the Lord and He answered me, and delivered me from all my fears"* (verse 4).

Because praise is so important a weapon in dispelling fear, not only is it imperative that we as parents learn to praise God continually; we need to teach our children to do likewise. Kookaburras are Australian birds that delight me no end with their boisterous laughter, and I could listen to them by the hour. Apparently though, the parent birds have to teach their young to make the sounds that are distinctive to them. God has made us to worship and serve Him, and if we are not doing both then we have fallen far short of God's intention for His creation.

Praise spontaneously flows to God when deliverance takes place as Isaiah prophesied concerning the ministry of Jesus Christ. *"To grant those who mourn in Zion, giving them a garland instead of ashes, the oil of gladness instead of mourning, the mantle of praise instead of a spirit of fainting"* ....(Isaiah 61:3).

These joyous words follow the declaration of deliverance from captivity, the words that Jesus quoted from Isaiah when He first commenced His public ministry (Isaiah 61:1; Luke 4:18).

As we learnt in the account of Paul and Silas, praise also ushers in deliverance; similarly praise enables us to maintain our deliverance and walk in it. If we are not praising Christians we are not victorious ones. It is as simple as that. No wonder we are encouraged to praise God continually. This is where speaking in tongues, the language of prayer and praise, is such a benefit to believers. Paul said: .... *"I shall pray with the spirit and I shall pray with the mind also; I shall sing with the spirit and I shall sing with the mind also"* (1 Corinthians 14:15).

One definition of praise is found in Hebrews 13:15: *"Through Him then (Jesus), let us continually offer up a sacrifice of praise to God, that is, the fruit of lips that give thanks to His name."*

7. Deal with Sin

Let us not think we can outsmart Satan if we become lax in our Christian walk and give way to the power of sin. The moment we deliberately deviate from the pathway of righteousness and pursue those attitudes or actions that are displeasing to God, we give the enemy ground to afflict us.

There is a principle of sowing and reaping that affects us all both positively and negatively. What we sow we reap, and we reap more than we sow. Jesus healed a bed-ridden man who had been thirty-eight years in his affliction. He later spoke to him and said, ..."*Behold, you have become well; do not sin any more, so that nothing worse may befall you*" (John 5:14). Surely the message is clear.

Recently I ministered to a young man who had been hospitalised for surgery. A temporary relief had been experienced but the disease was now spreading to other parts of the body. For many months he had struggled with both physical pain and the fear of what this disease could do to him. As we prayed, I discerned spirits of resentment. We stopped praying and talked at length about a longstanding animosity he held towards his father. After confessing his sin and renouncing the enemy, we continued our battle, this time against spirits of resentment as well as infirmity. The Lord desired to heal this young man, and that day an "axe was laid" to a root of bitterness which had given entrance for spirits of infirmity to attack his body. Just because we are sick or diseased does not mean we have sinned, but much infirmity has its origin with sin. "*Be angry, and yet do not sin; do not let the sun go down on your anger, and do not give the devil an opportunity."* (Literally: place.) Ephesians 4:26,27.

What do we do when we sin? Repent and confess (1 John 1:6—9).

8. Maintain a Confession of Freedom from Fear

Oh give thanks to the Lord, for He is good;
For His loving kindness is everlasting.
Let the redeemed of the Lord say so,
Whom He has redeemed from the hand of the
adversary.

Psalm 107:1,2

It is good to thank God for what He has done or is continuing to do for us. Our confession of liberty not only ascends to the Throne of God, but also impacts the powers of darkness, as well as bringing glory to God amongst His people.

Our very declaration of liberty from fear through Christ, acts as a wall of protection from demonic attack. Even if we are not completely free in an area of need, we still are to confess that we are free, in faith.

God changed Abram's name to Abraham before he had any descendants. Abram means "exalted father", while Abraham means "father of a multitude". Romans 4:17 says, *(as it is written, "A father of many nations have I made you")* *in the sight of Him whom he believed, even God, who gives life to the dead and calls into being that which does not exist.* (Literally: calls the things which do not exist as existing.)

Abraham was ninety nine years old and still childless

when God spoke to him and changed his name. However, his faith in God's Word was to release great blessing (Romans 4:18—24). As Abraham embraced the Word of God, faith was released in his heart. As he confessed what God had promised and praised Him for the fulfilment of it, Abraham grew in his faith, and, shortly afterwards, his son Isaac was born.

As the Word of God works in us releasing faith, as we, too, confess our liberty in Christ from all fear, calling those things that do not exist as existing, the power of God works in us to make reality our confessions of faith.

9. Be Christ-Centred

Paul, formerly known as Saul, was a Christ-rejecter, opposing both Jesus and His Church. However, one day he had a personal encounter with the resurrected Christ that transformed him. Years later he wrote:

But whatever things were gain to me, those things I have counted as loss for the sake of Christ.
More than that, I count all things to be loss in view of the surpassing value of knowing Christ Jesus my Lord, for whom I have suffered the loss of all things, and count them but rubbish in order that I may gain Christ.

Philippians 3:7,8

The example of Paul should inspire every Christian to be Christ-centred and to walk in such a way as to please God continually. Life is too short to focus on anything but that which is of eternal reality and consequence. We need Jesus in time and for eternity.

Jesus Christ is the Creator of the Universe (Colossians 1:16); He is the Saviour of the world (Acts 4:12); He is the Coming King (Revelation 1:7); He is the Judge of all men (Revelation 20:11—15). No one else in the history of time is worthy of our allegiance, our worship, and obedience; and He is the PRINCE OF PEACE (Isaiah 9:6).

By surrendering to His Lordship and gladly serving Him, we partake of the benefits of His Kingdom and can experience His peace. Let us always be Christ-centred. *"And the peace of God, which surpasses all comprehension, shall guard your heart and your minds in Christ Jesus"* (Philippians 4:7).

Attack and Counter-Attack

When our daughter Carrie was still only two years old, she experienced an onslaught of fear that greatly affected her for several weeks. Shirley and Carrie were shopping, when a person dressed in a bear costume, advertising a drive-in restaurant chain, stepped out of a doorway directly in front of them. At that time we were living in a wilderness area where the sighting of bears was common. To a two year old this bear was real. Carrie, suddenly overcome by fear, clung to her mother and screamed uncontrollably, while the person inside the bear costume laughed, not realising the spiritual significance of what was happening. Carrie's hysteria continued for sometime. There had been a major advantage taken by spirits of fear through this trauma.

Shirley understood the spiritual conflict we were in and that evil spirits use such occasions to bind; but she also knew the power of Jesus Christ to overcome the enemy, and immediately began to address those spirits of fear in Jesus' Name, binding their influence and commanding them to leave her.

The attack, however, had been a major one, and not one spirit had gained access into her life, but many. From that very hour our daughter developed fears for things that had never before worried her, such as a fear of the dark and a fear of noises.

Over the following weeks we took time to lay hands upon her and to launch the weapons of our warfare, by faith, declaring a total release from the effects of fear. Although there appeared no visible evidence of change, we knew the fears were weakening, simply because as we spoke to "the mountain" of fear, we believed that what we were saying was indeed happening. Our faith was in action and therefore the Spirit of God was at work. We knew the importance of perseverance.

A few weeks later Shirley and Carrie were walking near our home, when a skidder approached. Carrie reacted by gripping Shirley and screaming uncontrollably. Although the machine made much noise, Carrie had previously been unafraid of it. This, then, was a further manifestation of fear.

Becoming indignant — not at Carrie, but the enemy — Shirley led her in a confession that went something like this: "In the Name of Jesus I come against this fear. I break its power over my life. I refuse to be afraid. Fear has no place in me. You are leaving me now in Jesus' Name. Thank you Jesus for setting me free."

With that declaration from the lips of a child, and

as she repeated this confession for several minutes, the stronghold was finally broken, and from that day she returned to be herself once again. However, if as parents, we had not been alert and aware of the dimension of warfare we have been talking about, our daughter would still be bound to this day.

How wonderful it is to know that we can be set free from fear. More wonderful, however, is the experience of being set free and kept free by God's power.

If you will surrender your life to Jesus Christ and live for Him; if you will take up your spiritual weapons and begin launching them against the fears that grip you; if you will persevere in faith, believing that the Spirit of God is working with you to bring freedom, you will discover fears leaving you and a whole new dimension of life opening before you.

You will indeed experience the reality of walking fear free.

Chapter 12

Scriptures for Meditation

Psalm 3

O Lord, how my adversaries have increased!
Many are rising up against me.
Many are saying of my soul,
"There is no deliverance for him in God."

But Thou, O Lord, art a shield about me,
My glory, and the One who lifts my head.
I was crying to the Lord with my voice,
And He answered me from His holy mountain.

I lay down and slept;
I awoke, for the Lord sustains me.
I will not be afraid of ten thousands of people
Who have set themselves against me round about.

Arise, O Lord; save me, O my God!
For Thou hast smitten all my enemies on the cheek;
Thou hast shattered the teeth of the wicked.
Salvation belongs to the Lord;
Thy blessing be upon Thy people!

Psalm 27:1—6

The Lord is my light and my salvation;
Whom shall I fear?
The Lord is the defense of my life;
Whom shall I dread?

When evildoers came upon me to devour my flesh,
My adversaries and my enemies, they stumbled and
*   fell.*

Though a host encamp against me,
My heart will not fear;
Though war arise against me,
In spite of this I shall be confident.

One thing I have asked from the Lord, that I shall
*   seek;*
That I may dwell in the house of the Lord all the
*   days of my life,*
To behold the beauty of the Lord,
And to meditate in His temple.

For in the day of trouble He will conceal me in His
*   tabernacle;*
In the secret place of His tent He will hide me;
He will lift me up on a rock.

And now my head will be lifted up above my
*   enemies around me;*
And I will offer in His tent sacrifices with shouts of
*   joy;*
I will sing, yes, I will sing praises to the Lord.

Psalm 34:1—7

I will bless the Lord at all times;
His praise shall continually be in my mouth.
My soul shall make its boast in the Lord;
The humble shall hear it and rejoice.
O magnify the Lord with me,
And let us exalt His name together.

I sought the Lord, and He answered me,
And delivered me from all my fears.
They looked to Him and were radiant,
And their faces shall never be ashamed.
This poor man cried and the Lord heard him;
And saved him out of all his troubles.
The angel of the Lord encamps around those who
     fear Him,
And rescues them.

Psalm 118:1—17

Give thanks to the Lord, for He is good;
For His lovingkindness is everlasting.
Oh let Israel say,
"His lovingkindness is everlasting."
Oh let the house of Aaron say,
"His lovingkindness is everlasting."
Oh let those who fear the Lord say,
"His lovingkindness is everlasting."

From my distress I called upon the Lord;
The Lord answered me and set me in a large place.
The Lord is for me; I will not fear;

What can man do to me?
The Lord is for me among those who help me;
Therefore I shall look with satisfaction on those
who hate me.
It is better to take refuge in the Lord
Than to trust in man.
It is better to take refuge in the Lord
Than to trust in princes.

All nations surrounded me;
In the name of the Lord I will surely cut them off.
They surrounded me, yes, they surrounded me;
In the name of the Lord I will surely cut them off.
The surrounded me like bees;
They were extinguished as a fire of thorns;
In the name of the Lord I will surely cut them off.
You pushed me violently so that I was falling,
But the Lord helped me.
The Lord is my strength and song,
And He has become my salvation.

The sound of joyful shouting and salvation is in the
tents of the righteous;
The right hand of the Lord does valiantly.
The right hand of the Lord is exalted;
The right hand of the Lord does valiantly.
I shall not die, but live,
And tell of the works of the Lord.

Appendix

Simple and Complex Phobias

Following is a list of more than two hundred simple and complex phobias that have been classified with their medical names. Some phobias have more than one designation, but we have listed only one.

Acrophobia	fear of heights
Aerophobia	fear of flying
Agoraphobia	fear of open spaces
Agyiophobia	fear of streets
Aichmophobia	fear of pointed objects
Ailurophobia	fear of cats
Akousticophobia	fear of sound
Alcoholophobia	fear of alcoholism
Alektorophobia	fear of chickens
Algophobia	fear of pain
Amathophobia	fear of dust
Amychophobia	fear of being scratched
Androphobia	fear of men
Anemophobia	fear of wind
Anthophobia	fear of flowers
Anthrophobia	fear of people
Antlophobia	fear of flooding
Apeirophobia	fear of infinity
Apiphobia	fear of bees
Arachnophobia	fear of spiders
Asthenophobia	fear of weakness
Astraphobia	fear of lightning
Ataxiophobia	fear of disorder
Atelophobia	fear of imperfection

Atephobia	fear of ruin
Auroaphobia	fear of auroral lights
Automysophobia	fear of being dirty
Autophobia	fear of being alone
Bacilliphobia	fear of microbes
Bacteriophobia	fear of bacteria
Ballistophobia	fear of missiles
Barophobia	fear of gravity
Basiphobia	fear of walking
Bathophobia	fear of depth
Batrachophobia	fear of reptiles
Belonophobia	fear of sharp objects
Bibliophobia	fear of books
Brontophobia	fear of thunder
Cancerophobia	fear of cancer
Cardiophobia	fear of heart disease
Carnophobia	fear of meat
Cherophobia	fear of gaiety
Chionophobia	fear of snow
Cholerophobia	fear of cholera
Chromatophobia	fear of colours
Chrometophobia	fear of money
Chronophobia	fear of duration
Claustrophobia	fear of enclosed spaces
Cleptophobia	fear of stealing
Climacophobia	fear of climbing
Clinophobia	fear of going to bed
Cnidophobia	fear of stings
Coitophobia	fear of sexual intercourse
Coprophobia	fear of faeces
Cremnophobia	fear of precipices
Cryophobia	fear of ice
Crystallophobia	fear of glass
Cynophobia	fear of dogs
Demonophobia	fear of demons
Dendrophobia	fear of trees
Dermatosiophobia	fear of skin diseases
Dikephobia	fear of justice
Dipsophobia	fear of drinking
Domotophobia	fear of home
Doraphobia	fear of fur

Dysmorphophobia	fear of deformity
Ecclesiaphobia	fear of churches
Ecophobia	fear of home surroundings
Eisoptrophobia	fear of mirrors
Electrophobia	fear of electricity
Eleutherophobia	fear of freedom
Emetophobia	fear of vomiting
Entomophobia	fear of insects
Eosophobia	fear of dawn
Eremophobia	fear of solitude
Ereuthophobia	fear of blushing
Frigophobia	fear of the cold
Gamophobia	fear of marriage
Gephyrophobia	fear of crossing bridges
Graphophobia	fear of writing
Gymnophobia	fear of nakedness
Gynophobia	fear of women
Hadephobia	fear of Hell
Halophobia	fear of speaking
Hamartophobia	fear of sin
Haphephobia	fear of being touched
Harpaxophobia	fear of robbers
Hedonophobia	fear of pleasure
Heliophobia	fear of the sun
Helminthophobia	fear of worms
Hematophobia	fear of blood
Hierophobia	fear of sacred things
Hippophobia	fear of horses
Hodophobia	fear of travel
Homichlophobia	fear of fog
Homilophobia	fear of sermons
Hydrophobia	fear of water
Hygrophobia	fear of dampness
Hypengyophobia	fear of responsibility
Hypnophobia	fear of sleep
Hylephobia	fear of forests
Ichthyophobia	fear of fish
Ideophobia	fear of ideas
Iophobia	fear of rust
Kakorraphiaphobia	fear of failure
Katagelophobia	fear of ridicule

Kenophobia	fear of empty rooms
Kinesophobia	fear of motion
Laliophobia	fear of stuttering
Leprophobia	fear of leprosy
Limnophobia	fear of lakes
Linonophobia	fear of string
Logophobia	fear of words
Lyssophobia	fear of rabies
Maieusiophobia	fear of pregnancy
Maniaphobia	fear of insanity
Mastigophobia	fear of flogging
Mechanophobia	fear of machinery
Merinthophobia	fear of being bound
Metallophobia	fear of metal objects
Meteorophobia	fear of meteors
Microphobia	fear of germs
Musophobia	fear of mice
Mysophobia	fear of infection
Mythophobia	fear of making false statements
Necrophobia	fear of corpses
Neophobia	fear of change
Nephophobia	fear of clouds
Nomatophobia	fear of names
Nosemaphobia	fear of illness
Nosophobia	fear of disease
Nostophobia	fear of returning to home
Numerophobia	fear of numbers
Nyctophobia	fear of darkness
Ochlophobia	fear of crowds
Ochophobia	fear of vehicles
Odontophobia	fear of teeth
Odynephobia	fear of pain
Ombrophobia	fear of rain
Ommatophobia	fear of eyes
Oneirophobia	fear of dreams
Ophidiophobia	fear of snakes
Ornithophobia	fear of birds
Osmophobia	fear of odours
Ouranophobia	fear of Heaven
Panophobia	fear of everything
Paralipophobia	fear of neglect of duty

Parasitophobia	fear of parasites
Parthenophobia	fear of young girls
Patroiophobia	fear of heredity
Peccatophobia	fear of sinning
Pediculophobia	fear of lice
Pediophobia	fear of children
Peniaphobia	fear of poverty
Phagophobia	fear of swallowing
Pharmacophobia	fear of drugs
Phasmophobia	fear of ghosts
Phengophobia	fear of daylight
Phobophobia	fear of being afraid
Phonophobia	fear of speaking aloud
Photaugiaphobia	fear of glare
Photophobia	fear of light
Pnigerophobia	fear of smothering
Pnigophobia	fear of choking
Pogonophobia	fear of beards
Poinephobia	fear of punishment
Ponophobia	fear of fatigue
Potamophobia	fear of rivers
Potophobia	fear of drink
Polyphobia	fear of many things
Pteronophobia	fear of feathers
Pyrexiophobia	fear of fever
Pyrophobia	fear of fire
Rectophobia	fear of rectal disease
Rhabdophobia	fear of being beaten
Rhypophobia	fear of dirt
Satanophobia	fear of Satan
Scabiophobia	fear of itching
Scholionophobia	fear of school
Scopophobia	fear of being stared at
Selaphobia	fear of flashes
Siderodromophobia	fear of railways
Siderophobia	fear of stars
Sitophobia	fear of food
Spheksophobia	fear of wasps
Stasibasiphobia	fear of standing and walking
Stasiphobia	fear of standing upright
Tachophobia	fear of speed

Taphophobia	fear of being buried alive
Teratophobia	fear of monstrosities
Thaasophobia	fear of sitting idle
Thalassophobia	fear of the sea
Thanatophobia	fear of death
Theophobia	fear of God
Thermophobia	fear of heat
Tacophobia	fear of childbirth
Topophobia	fear of places
Toxicophobia	fear of poison
Traumatophobia	fear of injury
Trichophobia	fear of hair
Triskaidekaphobia	fear of thirteen
Trypanophobia	fear of inoculation
Tuberculophobia	fear of tuberculosis
Venereophobia	fear of venereal disease
Xenophobia	fear of strangers
Zelophobia	fear of jealousy
Zenophobia	fear of foreigners
Zoophobia	fear of animals

Christian Set Yourself Free

Graham and Shirley Powell

CHRISTIAN SET YOURSELF FREE is a Bible-based, inspirational teaching manual, that takes away the mystery and fear that often surrounds the ministry of deliverance.

It is designed to equip Christians with understanding as to how they can come into personal liberty as well as how to minister to others.

It is an ideal resource book for Pastors and Counsellors. Large format, 208 pages, price £4.95. (Published by New Wine Press, England).

Contents

Further information about all Sovereign World titles can be obtained from any of the following addresses:

Sovereign World (UK) Ltd
P O Box 17
Chichester PO20 6RY
England

Sovereign World (NZ) Ltd
P O Box 24-086
Royal Oak
AUCKLAND
New Zealand

Family Reading
3 College Street
Wendouree
Victoria 3355
Australia

Sovereign Books (Singapore) Pte Ltd
The Garden Hotel
14 Balmoral Road
SINGAPORE 1025

Books are normally supplied through bookshops. However, in the case of difficulty, please send payment to the appropriate address above and copies will be posted to you. Allow an extra 10% for postage. If you would like details of the Sovereign World Trust which sends books into Third World countries please write for a brochure to:

Sovereign World Trust
P O Box 777
Tonbridge
Kent RN9 2RU
England